CROCHET IMPKINS

CROCHET IMPKINS

STACKPOLE BOOKS

Essex, Connecticut
Blue Ridge Summit, Pennsylvania

MEGAN LAPP,
CREATOR OF CRAFTY INTENTIONS

STACKPOLE BOOKS

An imprint of The Globe Pequot Publishing Group, Inc.
64 South Main Street
Essex, CT 06426
www.globepequot.com

Distributed by NATIONAL BOOK NETWORK
800-462-6420

British Library Cataloguing in Publication Information available

Library of Congress Cataloging-in-Publication Data

Names: Lapp, Megan, 1984– author.
Title: Crochet impkins : over a million possible combinations! yes, really!
  / Megan Lapp.
Description: First edition. | Lanham : Stackpole Books, [2023] | Summary:
  "It is a wonderful thing to bring an Impkin to life with hook and yarn,
  and herein you will find the detailed instructions necessary to craft
  one, with an endless array of options for ears, antennae, hats, wings,
  tails, scales, horns, hairstyles, clothing, and accessories. Stitch by
  stitch, you'll cast a spell, until at last you have made a brand-new
  creature"— Provided by publisher.
Identifiers: LCCN 2023016452 (print) | LCCN 2023016453 (ebook) | ISBN
  9780811771603 (paperback) | ISBN 9780811771610 (epub)
Subjects: LCSH: Crocheting—Patterns. | Amigurumi—Patterns. | Soft toy
  making—Patterns. | Dollmaking.
Classification: LCC TT829 .L37 2023 (print) | LCC TT829 (ebook) | DDC
  746.43/4041—dc23/eng/20230419
LC record available at https://lccn.loc.gov/2023016452
LC ebook record available at https://lccn.loc.gov/2023016453

First Edition

CONTENTS

INTRODUCTION

Consider, friends, the Impkin. I'm sure you, just like all of us, have seen one out of the corner of your eye from time to time, racing from hiding place to nook or cranny. Odd little creatures of stitch and stuffing, of endless variety in form and manner . . . though usually a bit shy where most humans are concerned. They generally remain quite still when in view and only move about when they can do so freely without concerning their crafters or other human guests. But when they have the chance, they travel widely, diving into piles of yarn to pass into the space between or traveling through established stitchdoors, all to meet with each other in the Impkingdom hidden between the walls of the world. There they talk, share stories, sing, play, sometimes scrap, show off all the buttons and screws and pins and other amazing things they've collected, and ultimately return home before their crafters are ever aware they were gone.

Do they fill some niche in a secret ecology alongside other wee hidden beings? Do they have a whole society, with their own Imp King or Queen? Do they seek with intent, following the whims of the hearts their crafters granted them? Do they hope, dream, wish, smile, sing, play, and love? Are there other creatures like them?

The answers are, of course, yes, to each and every question, but I will not discuss them further here. After all, you did not seek out this book to learn all about Impkins' lifestyles or to find a taxonomy of their features or some hidden list of the names by which you might call them—those pages belong to other books. Instead, friend reader, you will find guidance on something far more important: the techniques and methods by which you might craft little stitchlings of your very own. So you stand at the beginning of a great and phenomenal journey.

It is a wonderful thing, I assure you, to bring an Impkin into life with hook and yarn. But from the outset, friend reader, do not allow yourself to be deceived by the physicality of the process. If there is only a single truth you glean from my words about the heart and nature of the Impkin, let it be this: the love and care and delight you hold within you while making your new diminutive friends are gifts you give to the Impkins and the source of the magic that brings them to life. Creating your Impkin is casting a spell one stitch at a time. That spell is powered by no arcane syllables or scintillating brew but by the hopes, dreams, and love that you pour into the little creatures.

This is why there is no single Impkin recipe, no singular path that always leads you to the same destination. Each and every Impkin is a reflection of their crafter, of the crafter's personality and imagination. No Impkins ever want anything more than to truly be themselves and to feel special in their crafter's eyes. The best thing you can do with these pages is to use all the advice and individual tools and components herein to craft the perfect Impkin *for you*, be it black or green or red or blue, be it one with horns, with a mushroom cap, with fins or scales or wings, or with any other feature you choose. The spell you cast depends on you discovering the true aspects of your own Impkin—for though these pages can guide you with countless tools to craft your own, the final decisions about which pieces to use can live only within your heart.

As you craft, let your hands and your heart guide you. Close your eyes, let the final form of your Impkin pass before your mind, and ask yourself about it. Did it have one horn or many? Did it have antennae? Did it have a snoot or a backpack? Allow the Impkin to reveal itself to you, and give it form with care!

Once you have crafted your Impkin, of course, you must live with them, caring for them and helping them as they need it. Each Impkin's needs are a little different: Impkins with antennae sometimes need help adjusting them to the appropriate frequency, while horned Impkins might need a periodic shave for their antlers, and fire-breathing Impkins will need you to help put a quick stop to any signs of smoke on their toes. Wandering Impkins can return home with holes or little stretched stitches, and it will be up to you to repair them. But know that all the effort is worth it; the gifts an Impkin brings to a home are far greater than any costs of repair.

So, my friend, embark on this journey with my blessing and the blessing of all the crafters who have walked the same wondrous path. We know the delights of the way before you, and we wish you to experience them with your whole heart. Whether you are creating a boisterous Impkin, who will greet you every morning as you wake, or a beautiful Impkin, who seems limned in a faint glow, or a mischievous Impkin, who seeks nothing more than to put a smile on your face, this journey will be marvelous and entirely your own. For creating an Impkin is nothing short of joyous magic, and let no one tell you differently.

Lyndella Mossgrove, Impologist Extraordinaire

P.S. Some credit must be given to the soul who assembled the patterns and instructions contained herein, of course, but I hope it's clear that I did the bulk of the imaginative and theoretical work, as an expert Impologist.

WHERE TO BEGIN

E ach Impkin is truly a unique individual. Throughout this book, you'll find examples with many of the options put together in various ways. Your choice of yarns and colors will further customize your creations. Use these examples as a jumping-off point for your own creativity. Do not be afraid to try new combinations!

To help you plan, each section, such as "Antennae" on page 31, includes a photo gallery that shows the available options for that attribute all in one place. Look through the book and note the options you'd like for your Impkin. Use the Planning Sheet on page 4 to design your Impkin and track your progress as you complete each piece.

Familiarize yourself with the Glossary of Terms and Stitches on page 5 to note any stitches or techniques that may be new to you, and refer to it as needed while you work.

YARN AND HOOK

I typically use a US size G (4 mm) crochet hook with a medium weight #4/worsted weight yarn (aran works as well). Not all yarn labels are completely standard on yarn weight. Some yarns are labeled worsted but feel more bulky; some yarns are labeled worsted but feel much lighter, like a DK weight yarn. When you crochet amigurumi, it is most important for your stitches to create a fabric that is tightly woven and will not show the fiberfill stuffing. You can use any weight yarn you want, but you must adjust your hook size accordingly so that the fabric of stitches is solid. I typically think of Red Heart, Big Twist, and Impeccable yarn in basic acrylic colors as good solid medium #4/worsted weight yarns. It is also important that you use the same weight yarn throughout the pattern so that all crocheted pieces of any particular pattern are made on the same scale (unless specifically instructed to use a different weight yarn for a particular piece).

Approximate yardage is given for each piece, but your needs will vary based on yarn choice and your individual crochet tension, so be sure to allow for a little extra if needed.

SIZE

An Impkin is approximately 7 in/17.75 cm tall from the feet to the top of the head, 4.5 in/11.5 cm wide from hand to hand, and 3 in/7.5 cm long from belly to back (not including ornamentation).

SAFETY EYES

I purchase safety eyes from two sources: Darkside Crochet and Suncatcher Craft Eyes. Darkside Crochet is UK based and Suncatcher is US based, but both ship anywhere you want. Both are also women-owned businesses. The eyes featured in this book are largely from Darkside Crochet, particularly the "Killer Kawaii" eyes.
You can find Darkside here: https://darksidecrochet.bigcartel.com
You can find Suncatcher here: https://suncatchercrafteyes.com

IMPKIN PLANNING SHEET

Here's an easy-to-use planning guide to copy, photograph, or scan and to use as a template for noting the styles and options you want for each Impkin you make.

IMPKIN BODY

Arm Style _____

Belly (for either Standing Body Style) _____

Body Style _____

BODY FEATURES

Antennae _____

Belly _____

Ears _____

Face Option _____

Hat or Hairstyle _____

Horns or Antlers _____

Scales _____

Tail _____

Wings _____

CLOTHING AND ACCESSORIES

Clothing _____

Neck Ornamentation _____

Accessory _____

GLOSSARY OF TERMS AND STITCHES

T o create the creatures in this book, you will need to learn a few possibly new-to-you stitches, particularly increases and decreases. The processes will be familiar, but where you work the stitches is important to note. Below is a list of terms and abbreviations for stitches that you should become familiar with and refer to as needed as you work the patterns.

[Brackets]	Brackets that come after BLO or FLO are used to indicate that these stitches are worked into the back loop only or front loop only. Ex.: BLO [SC 6] Brackets at the end of the row indicate the stitch count for the row. Ex.: [6]; this means there are 6 stitches in the row.
&	Located between two stitches, the "&" indicates that both stitches are made into the same stitch, as an increase, but with two different types of stitches. Go here for video demonstration: https://www.youtube.com/watch?v=jGA2nAzL2cU&t=16s
< or >	Indicates the stitch will start (<) or finish (>) in the same stitch as the last stitch or the next stitch.
<Dec>	Beginning in the SAME stitch as your last stitch, make a decrease stitch into that and the next stitch, and then, into the same stitch that the decrease stitch ends in, begin your next stitch. Go here for video demonstration: https://www.youtube.com/watch?v=Ni2ZM1cXJI4
2 Dec in 3 SC	Make one decrease as normal, and then make the second decrease starting in the SAME stitch as the first decrease and ending in the next stitch. Go here for video demonstration: https://www.youtube.com/watch?v=vWRuWd689KQ&t=4s
BLO [ ]	Back Loop Only ---- *NOTE: The rows with FLO or BLO stitches will be structured with brackets [ ]. The brackets will enclose any and all stitches that the FLO or BLO instruction should apply to. Ex: "BLO [SC 3], SC 3" would mean 3 single crochet stitches in the BLO and then 3 normal single crochet.*
Ch	Chain
Colorwork	When switching colors at the end of a row, switch to the new color when you make the slip stitch join. When you make the final yarn over to slip stitch at the end of the row, use the new color to do that final yarn over, and then chain 1; this creates a seamless transition to the new color.

DC	Double Crochet
DC Dec	YO (see below), insert into next stitch, YO, pull up, YO, pull through 2 loops, YO, insert into next stitch, YO, pull up, YO, pull through 2 loops, YO, pull through all 3 loops
DC/HDC Dec	YO, insert into next stitch, YO, pull up, YO, pull through 2 loops, YO, insert into next stitch, YO, pull up, YO, pull through all 4 loops
Dec	Decrease: One stitch combining 2 spaces. All decreases are single crochet decreases unless otherwise stated.
FLO [ ]	Front Loop Only *NOTE: The rows with FLO or BLO stitches will be structured with brackets [ ]. The brackets will enclose any and all stitches that the FLO or BLO instruction should apply to. Ex: "FLO [SC 3], SC 3" would mean 3 single crochet stitches in the FLO and then 3 normal single crochet.*
FP HDC	Front Post Half Double Crochet YO, insert hook from front to back to front around post of corresponding stitch below, YO, pull up, YO, pull through all remaining loops
FP Triple Crochet	Front Post Triple Crochet YO twice, insert hook from front to back around post of the next available stitch, YO, pull up, (YO and pull through 2 loops) x 3, skip the stitch behind the FP Triple Crochet
Half Trip	Half Triple Crochet YO twice, insert into next stitch, YO, pull up, YO, pull through 2 loops, YO, pull through all remaining loops
Half Trip Dec	Half Triple Crochet Decrease YO twice, insert into next stitch, YO, pull up, YO, pull through 2 loops, YO twice, insert into next stitch, YO, pull up, YO, pull through 2 loops, YO, pull through all remaining loops
Half Trip Inc	Half Triple Crochet Increase Two Half Trip stitches into the same stitch
HDC	Half Double Crochet YO, insert hook into next stitch, YO, pull up, YO, pull through all 3 loops
HDC Dec	Half Double Crochet Decrease YO, insert into next stitch, YO, pull up, YO, pull through 2 loops, YO, insert into next stitch, YO, pull up, YO, pull through all 4 loops
HDC/SC Dec	Half Double Crochet and Single Crochet Decrease YO, insert into next stitch, YO, pull up, YO, pull through 2 loops, insert into next stitch, YO, pull up, YO, pull through all 3 loops
Inc	Increase, 2 stitches in one space Assume all increases are SC increases unless otherwise specified.

OC	Original Chain This refers to the very first set of chain stitches you made to start the piece you're working on.
Picot	Ch 2, Sl St in the second chain from hook (picot stitches are not included in the stitch counts)
Right side/ Outside vs. Wrong side/ Inside	To crochet right-side out, you will insert your hook from the outside/right side of the work to the inside/wrong side of the work, and if you are right-handed, you will be working in a clockwise direction. Here is a video on this technique: https://www.youtube.com/watch?v=beReNFWQPAs
SC	Single Crochet
SC/HDC Dec	Single Crochet/Half Double Crochet Decrease Insert into next stitch, YO, pull up, YO, insert into next stitch, YO, pull up, YO, pull through all remaining loops Here is a video on this stitch: https://www.youtube.com/watch?v=h4wkxMOMqXg&t=12s
SC/HDC/SC Dec	Single Crochet/Half Double Crochet/Single Crochet Decrease Insert into next stitch, YO, pull up, YO, insert into next stitch, YO, pull up, YO, pull through 2 loops, insert into next stitch, YO, pull up, YO, pull through all remaining loops
Sl St	Slip Stitch
Sl St to beginning stitch, Ch 1	JOINING: Most of the patterns are written with a "Slip Stitch, Chain 1" joining method for each row. This DOES affect the shape of each piece but in a minor way, as the piece was written with the seam shift in mind. If you prefer to crochet in spiral/in the round, you are welcome to try it, but I do not guarantee that all asymmetrical sections will come out exactly as shown. To end the row, after you have worked the entire row, you will slip stitch into the first stitch you worked in that row, and then Chain 1. The first stitch of the next row should be worked into the same stitch that you slip stitched into. For video demonstration, go here: https://www.youtube.com/watch?v=Qqu5N7TCt3U
St	Stitch
Triple Crochet	YO twice, insert into next stitch, YO, pull up, YO, pull through 2 loops, YO, pull through 2 loops, YO, pull through all remaining loops
Triple SC Dec	Triple Single Crochet Decrease One stitch combining 3 spaces using single crochet (Insert in next stitch space, YO, pull up) x 3, YO, pull through all 4 loops
Triple SC Inc	Triple Single Crochet Increase Three single crochet stitches in 1 space
Triple DC Inc	Triple Double Crochet Increase Three Double Crochet Stitches in 1 space
YO	Yarn Over

IMPKIN BODY STYLES

For your Impkin's body, you have four options: two for a standing Impkin and two for a sitting Impkin. If your Impkin is standing (for either standing body style), you'll also make the belly. There are two arm styles, which you should choose and make first, as they will attach to your body as you crochet.

Arm Style 1

Arm Style 2

Belly, used with Standing Body Styles 1 and 2

Standing Body Style 1

Standing Body Style 2

Sitting Body Style 1

Sitting Body Style 2

ARM STYLE 1 (MAKE 2)

Main Body Color Yarn: Approximately 16 yd/14.75 m total

1. SC 6 in Magic Circle, Sl St to beginning stitch, Ch 1 [6]
2. (SC, Inc, SC) x 2, Sl St to beginning stitch, Ch 1 [8]
3. SC 8, Sl St to beginning stitch, Ch 1 [8]
4. SC 8, Sl St to beginning stitch, Ch 1 [8]
5. SC 3, Dec, SC 3, Sl St to beginning stitch, Ch 1 [7]
6. Dec, SC 5, Sl St to beginning stitch, Ch 1 [6]
7. SC 4, Dec, Sl St to beginning stitch, Ch 1 [5]
8. SC 5, Sl St to beginning stitch, Ch 1 [5]
9. SC 5, Sl St to beginning stitch, Ch 1 [5]
10. SC 5, Sl St to beginning stitch [5]

Fasten off with short yarn tail; tuck this tail into the arm. Stuff very lightly with fiberfill or not at all. The arms in the photos are not stuffed.

ARM STYLE 2 (MAKE 2)

Main Body Color Yarn: Approximately 20 yd/18.25 m total

1. SC 6 in Magic Circle, Sl St to beginning stitch, Ch 1 [6]
2. (SC, Inc) x 3, Sl St to beginning stitch, Ch 1 [9]
3. SC 9, Sl St to beginning stitch, Ch 1 [9]
4. SC 9, Sl St to beginning stitch, Ch 1 [9]
5. SC 9, Sl St to beginning stitch, Ch 1 [9]
6. Dec, SC 7, Sl St to beginning stitch, Ch 1 [8]
7. SC 3, Dec, SC 3, Sl St to beginning stitch, Ch 1 [7]
8. SC 5, Dec, Sl St to beginning stitch, Ch 1 [6]
9. SC 2, Dec, SC 2, Sl St to beginning stitch, Ch 1 [5]
10. SC 5, Sl St to beginning stitch, Ch 1 [5]
11. SC 5, Sl St to beginning stitch, Ch 1 [5]
12. SC 5, Sl St to beginning stitch [5]

Fasten off with short yarn tail; tuck this tail into the arm. Stuff very lightly with fiberfill or not at all. The arms in the photos are not stuffed.

BELLY (FOR STANDING BODY STYLE 1 OR STYLE 2)

Main Body Color Yarn: Approximately 1 yd/1 m total

If you are using a variegated yarn to make the body, then it is recommended that you make the Belly piece after you create the first leg of the Impkin Body.

In Magic Circle, SC 2, HDC 2, SC 2, HDC 2, Sl St to beginning stitch [8]

Fasten off with short yarn tail. Put a stitch marker in the third stitch.

STANDING BODY STYLE 1

**Main Body Color Yarn:
Approximately 41 yd/37.5 m total**

1. In Magic Circle: SC 2, HDC 3, SC 2, Sl St to beginning stitch, Ch 1 [7]

2. BLO [SC 7], Sl St to beginning stitch, Ch 1 [7]

3. SC 2, SC/HDC/SC Dec, SC 2, Sl St to beginning stitch, Ch 1 [5]

4. SC 5, Sl St to beginning stitch, Ch 1 [5]

5. Inc, SC 4, Sl St to beginning stitch, Ch 1 [6]

6. SC 4, <Dec>, SC 2, Sl St to beginning stitch, Ch 1 [7]

7. SC 4, Inc, SC 2, Sl St to beginning stitch [8]

Fasten off with short yarn tail. This completes Leg #1.

> When creating an Impkin, the feet will not be facing straight forward. They are intentionally designed to be slightly splayed.

For Leg #2, start again from Row 1, Ch 1 at the end of Row 7, and continue to Row 8.

8. SC, Ch 2, starting into the first stitch from Row 7 on Leg #1, SC 8, SC in each of the 2 chain stitches between the legs, continuing into the next available stitch on Leg #2, SC 7, Sl St to beginning stitch, Ch 1 [18]

> Do not work into the Sl St join from Leg #1.

9. Inc, SC 2 (in the Ch 2), Inc, SC 6, starting by working into the marked stitch on the belly and the next available stitch on the body at the same time, SC 4, continuing in the next available stitch on the body only, SC 6, Sl St to beginning stitch, Ch 1 [22]

> When you work into the belly piece, insert your hook into the wrong side/inside of the belly piece first, then insert your hook into the right side/outside of the body next, and complete a SC through both at the same time. Do not work into the Sl St join from the Belly piece. See this video for more information on this technique: https://youtu.be/paLzlAi--vk

10. Inc, SC, Dec, SC, Inc, SC 6; starting in the same stitch that you first worked into on the belly piece ONLY, SC 6 (you will finish in the same stitch you last crocheted into on the Belly), SC 6, Sl St to beginning stitch, Ch 1 [25]

> In this row, when you work into the same stitch that you already worked into on the belly, you will work into the belly stitch only. Do not work into the stitch that was made to attach the belly to the body; work into the belly piece itself.

11. SC 25, Sl St to beginning stitch, Ch 1 [25]

12. SC 2, start a Dec stitch, Skip a stitch, complete the Dec into the next available stitch, SC 20, Sl St to beginning stitch, Ch 1 [23]

13. SC 23, Sl St to beginning stitch, Ch 1 [23]

14. SC 23, Sl St to beginning stitch, Ch 1 [23]

15. SC 11, Dec, SC 4, Dec, SC 4, Sl St to beginning stitch, Ch 1 [21]

16. SC 10, Dec, SC 5, Dec, SC 2, Sl St to beginning stitch, Ch 1 [19]

17. SC 2, 2 Dec in 3 SC, SC 14, Sl St to beginning stitch, Ch 1 [18]

18. (SC 2, Dec, SC 2) x 3, Sl St to beginning stitch, Ch 1 [15]

19. (SC 3, Dec) x 3, Sl St to beginning stitch, Ch 1 [12]

20. SC 12, Sl St to beginning stitch, Ch 1 [12]

You can begin to stuff the body medium-firm with fiberfill stuffing all the way down to the feet. Continue to stuff as you go. If you are going to use a hat of some kind, or if you want the head to be well supported, leave some room in the body to insert a wire. For this project, I recommend a 0.3 in/0.75 cm diameter foam flexible curling rod. It is wired on the inside, and you can insert it into the neck of the Impkin. This will support the head under the weight of a hat, and the foam will protect the crochet work from the wire.

21. SC in the first stitch on Arm #1 and the first available stitch on the Body, SC in the next available stitch on the Arm and the next available stitch on the Body—working in the Body only—SC 2, SC in the last stitch on Arm #2 and the next available stitch on the body, SC in the next available stitch on the Arm and the next available stitch on the Body—working in the Body only—SC, Dec, SC, Dec, SC in the Body only of the same stitch as the first stitch into Arm #1, continue in spiral, DO NOT Sl St, Ch 1 [11]

When you work into the arm piece, insert your hook into the wrong side/inside of the arm first, then insert your hook into the right side/outside of the body next, and complete a SC through both at the same time. Do not work into the Sl St join from the Arms.

22. Starting in the first available stitch on the Arm, SC 3 around the outer edge of Arm #1—ignoring the stitches you used to attach the arm—SC 2, SC 3 around the outer edge of Arm #2—ignoring the stitches you used to attach the arm—Dec, SC, Dec.

In this row, when you work into the Arms, only crochet around the outside available stitches on the Arms; ignore the stitches that you made to connect the Arm with the Body in Row 21.

23. (Dec, SC) x 2, Dec, Triple SC Dec [6]

24. FLO [Inc x 6] [12]

25. (SC, Inc) x 6 [18]

26. (SC, Inc, SC) x 6 [24]

27. (SC 3, Inc) x 6 [30]

28. (SC 2, Inc, SC 2) x 6 [36]

29. SC 36 [36]

30. SC 36 [36]

31. SC 29, Dec, SC, Dec, SC, Dec [33]

This row goes 1 stitch beyond where it started, and you work 34 stitches, but there are only 33 available for the next row.

32. Dec, SC, Dec, SC, Dec, SC 25 [30]

33. SC 30 [30]

34. SC 30 [30]

35. SC 30 [30]

36. (SC 4, Dec) x 5 [25]

Insert 12 mm or 15 mm black safety eyes OR 18 mm or 23 mm colored iris safety eyes at the front of the face just above the decreases you worked in Rows 31 and 32 (or 1 row above that), with 3 or 4 stitch spaces between the eye posts. (The post will be inserted in a stitch space [a space between two stitch posts], and then you count 3–4 stitch spaces away from the post, and insert the next eye post into the next available stitch space.) Insert the eyes and then check to see if you like the placement before fastening them in place; adjust as necessary. If you are using a foam curling rod and/or wire, you can insert it at this point.

37. (SC 3, Dec) x 5 [20]

38. (SC, Dec, SC) x 5 [15]

39. (SC, Dec) x 5 [10]

40. Dec x 5 [5]

Fasten off with 12 in/30.5 cm yarn tail. Use the yarn tail to sew shut the hole in the top of the head. Weave in ends.

Standing Body Style 1, Arm Style 1, Antennae Style 1

STANDING BODY STYLE 2

Main Body Color Yarn:
Approximately 47 yd/43 m total

1. In Magic Circle: SC 6, Sl St to beginning stitch, Ch 1 [6]

2. Inc x 2, HDC Inc x 2, Inc x 2 Sl St to beginning stitch, Ch 1 [12]

3. BLO [SC 12], Sl St to beginning stitch, Ch 1 [12]

4. SC 4, HDC Dec x 2, SC 4, Sl St to beginning stitch, Ch 1 [10]

5. SC 3, HDC Dec x 2, SC 3, Sl St to beginning stitch, Ch 1 [8]

6. SC 3, Dec, SC 3, Sl St to beginning stitch, Ch 1 [7]

7. SC 7, Sl St to beginning stitch, Ch 1 [7]

8. SC 3, Inc, SC 3, Sl St to beginning stitch [8]

Fasten off with short yarn tail. This completes Leg #1.

For Leg #2, start again from Row 1, Ch 1 at the end of Row 8, and continue to Row 9.

9. SC 2, Ch 2, starting into the first stitch from Row 8 on Leg #1, SC 8, SC in each of the 2 chain stitches between the Legs, continuing into the next available stitch on Leg #2, SC 6, Sl St to beginning stitch, Ch 1 [18]

> Do not work into the Sl St join from Leg #1.

> When creating an Impkin, the feet will not be facing straight forward. They are intentionally designed to be slightly splayed.

10. SC, Inc, SC 2 (in the Ch 2), Inc, SC 6, starting by working into the marked stitch on the Belly and the next available stitch on the Body at the same time, SC 4, continuing in the next available stitch on the Body only, SC 5, Sl St to beginning stitch, Ch 1 [22]

> When you work into the Belly piece, insert your hook into the wrong side/inside of the Belly piece first, then insert your hook into the right side/outside of the Body next, and complete a SC through both at the same time. Do not work into the Sl St join from the Belly piece. See this video for more information on this technique: https://youtu.be/paLzlAi--vk

Standing Body Style 2, Arm Style 2, Hood and Cape

11. SC, Inc, SC, Dec, SC, Inc, SC 6, starting in the same stitch that you first worked into on the Belly piece ONLY, SC 6 (you will finish in the same stitch you last crocheted into on the Belly), continuing into the next available stitch on the body, SC 5, Sl St to beginning stitch, Ch 1 [25]

In this row, when you work into the same stitch that you already worked into on the Belly, you will work into the Belly stitch only. Do not work into the stitch that was made to attach the Belly to the Body; work into the Belly piece itself.

12. SC 25, Sl St to beginning stitch, Ch 1 [25]

13. SC 3, start a Dec stitch, skip 1 stitch, complete the Dec into the next available stitch, SC 19, Sl St to beginning stitch, Ch 1 [23]

14. SC 23, Sl St to beginning stitch, Ch 1 [23]

15. SC 23, Sl St to beginning stitch, Ch 1 [23]

16. SC 12, Dec, SC 4, Dec, SC 3, Sl St to beginning stitch, Ch 1 [21]

17. SC 11, Dec, SC 5, Dec, SC, Sl St to beginning stitch, Ch 1 [19]

18. SC 3, 2 Dec in 3 SC, SC 13, Sl St to beginning stitch, Ch 1 [18]

19. (SC 2, Dec, SC 2) x 3, Sl St to beginning stitch, Ch 1 [15]

20. (SC 3, Dec) x 3, Sl St to beginning stitch, Ch 1 [12]

21. SC 12, Sl St to beginning stitch, Ch 1 [12]

You can begin to stuff the body medium-firm with fiberfill stuffing all the way down to the feet. Continue to stuff as you go. If you are going to use a hat of some kind, or if you want the head to be well supported, leave some room in the body to insert a wire. For this project, I recommend 0.3 in/ 0.75 cm diameter foam flexible curling rod. It is wired on the inside, and you can insert it into the neck of the Impkin. This will support the head under the weight of a hat, and the foam will protect the crochet work from the wire.

Standing Body
Style 2,
Arm Style 2,
Mandrake Topper

22. SC, SC in the first stitch on Arm #1 and the first available stitch on the Body, SC in the next available stitch on the Arm and the next available stitch on the Body—working in the Body only—SC 2, SC in the last stitch on Arm #2 and the next available stitch on the Body, SC in the next available stitch on the Arm and the next available stitch on the Body—working in the Body only—SC, Dec, SC, Dec, SC in the first stitch you used to attach Arm #1 to the body, continue in spiral, DO NOT Sl St, Ch 1 [11]

23. Starting in the first available stitch on the Arm, SC 3 around the outer edge of Arm #1—ignoring the stitches you used to attach the Arm—SC 2, SC 3 around the outer edge of Arm #2—ignoring the stitches you used to attach the arm—Dec, SC, Dec [11]

When you work into the Arm piece, insert your hook into the wrong side/inside of the Arm first, then insert your hook into the right side/outside of the Body next, and complete a SC through both at the same time. Do not work into the Sl St join from the Arms. The last Dec of this row will finish into the first stitch you worked in this row. The last SC in this row will be worked into the first stitch that you used to attach Arm #1 to the Body.

In this row, when you work into the Arms, only crochet around the outside available stitches on the Arms; ignore the stitches that you made to connect the Arm with the Body in Row 22.

Standing Body Style 2, Arm Style 2, Round Mushroom Cap

24. (Dec, SC) x 2, Dec, Triple SC Dec [6]

25. FLO [Inc x 6] [12]

26. (SC, Inc) x 6 [18]

27. (SC, Inc, SC) x 6 [24]

28. (SC 3, Inc) x 6 [30]

29. (SC 2, Inc, SC 2) x 6 [36]

30. SC 36 [36]

31. SC 36 [36]

32. SC 29, Dec, SC, Dec, SC, Dec [33]

> This row goes 1 stitch beyond where it started. In this row, you work 34 stitches, but there are only 33 available for the next row.

33. Dec, SC, Dec, SC, Dec, SC 25 [30]

34. SC 30 [30]

35. SC 30 [30]

36. SC 30 [30]

37. (SC 4, Dec) x 5 [25]

> Insert 12 mm or 15 mm black safety eyes OR 18 mm or 23 mm colored iris safety eyes at the front of the face just above (or 1 row above) the decreases you worked in Rows 32 and 33, with 3 or 4 stitch spaces between the eye posts. (The post will be inserted in a stitch space [a space between two stitch posts], and then you count 3–4 stitch spaces away from the post, and insert the next eye post into the next available stitch space.) Insert the eyes and then check to see if you like the placement before fastening them in place; adjust as necessary. If you are using a foam curling rod and/or wire, you can insert it at this point.

38. (SC 3, Dec) x 5 [20]

39. (SC, Dec, SC) x 5 [15]

40. (SC, Dec) x 5 [10]

41. Dec x 5 [5]

Fasten off with 12 in/30.5 cm yarn tail. Use the yarn tail to sew shut the hole in the top of the head. Weave in ends.

Sitting Body
Style 1, Arm Style 2,
Feather Topper,
Bird Tail,
Feather Wings

SITTING BODY STYLE 1

NOTE: The sitting Impkin may tip over without support. You can add items such as glass gems or poly beads to weight the bottom of the body and add stability. Sitting Style 2 has longer legs and tends to be more innately stable than Sitting Style 1.

Main Body Color Yarn:
Approximately 41 yd/37.5 m total

Leg Instructions

1. In Magic Circle: SC 2, HDC 3, SC 2, Sl St to beginning stitch, Ch 1 [7]

2. BLO [SC 7], Sl St to beginning stitch, Ch 1 [7]

3. SC 2, SC/HDC/SC Dec, SC 2, Sl St to beginning stitch, Ch 1 [5]

4. SC 5, Sl St to beginning stitch, Ch 1 [5]

5. SC 2, Inc, SC 2, Sl St to beginning stitch, Ch 1 [6]

6. SC 3, <Dec>, SC 3, Sl St to beginning stitch, Ch 1 [7]

7. SC 3, Inc, SC 3, Sl St to beginning stitch [8]

Fasten off with a short yarn tail. This completes Leg #1. Repeat these instructions to create Leg #2. Fasten off with a short yarn tail, and then continue to the Sitting Body instructions.

Sitting Body Style 1 Instructions

1. SC 6 in Magic Circle, Sl St to beginning stitch, Ch 1 [6]

2. Inc x 6, Sl St to beginning stitch, Ch 1 [12]

3. (SC, Inc) x 6, Sl St to beginning stitch, Ch 1 [18]

4. SC, Inc, SC 3, starting into the second stitch from Row 7 on Leg #1 and the next available stitch on the Body at the same time, SC 3, continuing into the next available stitch on the Body only, SC 2, starting into the second stitch from Row 7 on Leg #2 and the next available stitch on the Body at the same time, SC 3, continuing into the next available stitch on the Body only, SC 3, Inc, SC, Sl St to beginning stitch, Ch 1 [20]

When you work into the Legs, insert your hook into the wrong side/inside of the Leg piece first, then insert your hook into the right side/outside of the Body next, and complete a SC through both at the same time. Do not work into the Sl St join from the Leg piece. See this video for more information on this technique: https://youtu.be/paLzlAi--vk

5. SC, Inc, SC 3, starting in the last available stitch on the Body and finishing in the first available stitch on the Leg, work a Dec, working in the Leg only SC 3, starting in the last available stitch on the Leg and finishing in the first available stitch in the Body, work a Decrease, SC in the same stitch that the last Decrease ended in, <Dec>, SC, start a Decrease in the same stitch as your last SC, and complete the Decrease in the first available stitch on the next Leg, working in the Leg only, SC 3, starting in the last available stitch on the Leg and finishing in the first available stitch in the Body, work a Decrease, SC 3, Inc, SC, Sl St to beginning stitch, Ch 1 [25]

When you work into the Legs in this row, you will always be working as normal, inserting your hook from the outside/right side to the inside/wrong side of the Leg to complete the stitches, and you will ignore all the stitches that were used to connect the Leg and the Body in the previous row.

6. SC, Dec, SC 7, Inc, SC 3, Inc, SC 7, Dec, SC, Sl St to beginning stitch, Ch 1 [25]

7. SC 25, Sl St to beginning stitch, Ch 1 [25]

8. Dec, SC 21, Dec, Sl St to beginning stitch, Ch 1 [23]

9. SC 23, Sl St to beginning stitch, Ch 1 [23]

10. SC 9, Dec, SC 4, Dec, SC 6, Sl St to beginning stitch, Ch 1 [21]

When you work on a sitting Impkin, the way that you stuff the piece will affect the stability of its sitting position. Do not overstuff the Legs. As you stuff the feet and Body, pay attention to the sitting position to ensure that it sits flat on a flat surface. The first picture is incorrectly stuffed; the second picture is correctly stuffed. (These photos are meant to illustrate the example, but they feature Body Style 2.)

11. SC 5, Dec, SC 10, Dec, SC 2, Sl St to beginning stitch, Ch 1 [19]

12. Dec, SC 17, Sl St to beginning stitch, Ch 1 [18]

13. (SC 2, Dec, SC 2) x 3, Sl St to beginning stitch, Ch 1 [15]

14. (SC 3, Dec) x 3, Sl St to beginning stitch, Ch 1 [12]

Sitting Body
Style 1,
Arm Style 1,
Pumpkin Stem
Cap

You can begin to stuff the body medium-firm with fiberfill stuffing.
Continue to stuff as you go. If you are going to use a hat of some kind, or if
you want the head to be well supported, leave some room in the body to
insert a wire. For this project, I recommend a 0.3 in/0.75 cm diameter foam
flexible curling rod. It is wired on the inside, and you can insert it into
the neck of the Impkin. This rod will support the head under the weight
of a hat and protect the crochet work from the wire with the foam of the
curler. If you are adding weight (using glass gems, poly beads, etc.), add it
now before you add fiberfill.

15. SC 2, SC in the first stitch on Arm
#1 and the first available stitch on
the Body, SC in the next available
stitch on the Arm and the next
available stitch on the Body—
working in the Body only—SC,
Dec, SC, Dec, SC, SC in the first
stitch on Arm #2 and the same
stitch you worked the last SC stitch
into on the Body, SC in the next
available stitch on the Arm and the
last available stitch on the Body,
continue in spiral, DO NOT Sl St,
Ch 1 [11]

When you work into the Arm
piece, insert your hook into the
wrong side/inside of the Arm
first, then insert your hook into
the right side/outside of the
Body next, and complete a SC
through both at the same time.
Do not work into the Sl St join
from the Arms.

16. SC 2, starting in the first available stitch on the Arm, SC 3 around the outer edge of Arm #1—ignoring the stitches you used to attach the Arm, working in the Body only—Dec, SC, Dec, SC 3 around the outer edge of Arm #2—ignoring the stitches you used to attach the Arm [11]

In this row, when you work into the Arms, only crochet around the outside available stitches on the Arms; ignore the stitches that you made to connect the Arm with the Body in the previous row.

17. Dec, SC, Dec, Triple SC Dec, Dec, SC [6]

18. FLO [Inc x 6] [12]
19. (SC, Inc) x 6 [18]
20. (SC, Inc, SC) x 6 [24]
21. (SC 3, Inc) x 6 [30]
22. (SC 2, Inc, SC 2) x 6 [36]
23. SC 36 [36]
24. SC 36 [36]

25. SC 36 [36]
26. SC 16, (Dec, SC, Dec, SC, Dec) x 2, SC 4 [30]
27. SC 30 [30]
28. SC 30 [30]
29. SC 30 [30]
30. (SC 4, Dec) x 5 [25]

Insert 12 mm or 15 mm black safety eyes OR 18 mm or 23 mm colored iris safety eyes at the front of the face just above (or 1 row above) the decreases you worked in Row 26 with 3 or 4 stitch spaces between the eye posts. (The post will be inserted in a stitch space [a space between two stitch posts], and then you count 3–4 stitch spaces away from the post, and insert the next eye post into the next available stitch space.) Insert the eyes and then check to see if you like the placement before fastening them in place; adjust as necessary. If you are using a foam curling rod and/or wire, you can insert it at this point.

31. (SC 3, Dec) x 5 [20]
32. (SC, Dec, SC) x 5 [15]
33. (SC, Dec) x 5 [10]
34. Dec x 5 [5]

Fasten off with 12 in/30.5 cm yarn tail. Use the yarn tail to sew shut the hole in the top of the head. Weave in ends.

SITTING BODY STYLE 2

NOTE: The sitting Impkin Body is not always stable sitting by itself. To increase stability, you can optionally fill the bottom of the body with some weight, like glass gems or alternative weight. Style 2 has longer legs and tends to be more innately stable than Style 1.

Main Body Color Yarn: Approximately 46 yd/42 m total

Leg Instructions

1. In Magic Circle: SC 6, Sl St to beginning stitch, Ch 1 [6]

2. Inc x 2, HDC Inc x 2, Inc x 2, Sl St to beginning stitch, Ch 1 [12]

3. BLO [SC 12], Sl St to beginning stitch, Ch 1 [12]

4. SC 4, HDC Dec x 2, SC 4, Sl St to beginning stitch, Ch 1 [10]

5. SC 3, HDC Dec x 2, SC 3, Sl St to beginning stitch, Ch 1 [8]

6. SC 3, Dec, SC 3, Sl St to beginning stitch, Ch 1 [7]

7. SC 7, Sl St to beginning stitch, Ch 1 [7]

8. SC 3, Inc, SC 3, Sl St to beginning stitch [8]

Fasten off with a short yarn tail. This completes Leg #1. Repeat these instructions to create Leg #2; fasten off with a short yarn tail, and then continue to the Sitting Body instructions.

Sitting Body Style 2 Instructions

1. SC 6 in Magic Circle, Sl St to beginning stitch, Ch 1 [6]

2. Inc x 6, Sl St to beginning stitch, Ch 1 [12]

3. (SC, Inc) x 6, Sl St to beginning stitch, Ch 1 [18]

4. SC, Inc, SC 3, starting into the second stitch from Row 8 on Leg #1 and the next available stitch on the Body at the same time, SC 3, continuing into the next available stitch on the Body only, SC 2, starting into the second stitch from Row 8 on Leg #2 and the next available stitch on the body at the same time, SC 3, continuing into the next available stitch on the body only, SC 3, Inc, SC, Sl St to beginning stitch, Ch 1 [20]

> When you work into the Legs, insert your hook into the wrong side/inside of the Leg piece first, then insert your hook into the right side/outside of the Body next, and complete a SC through both at the same time. Do not work into the Sl St join from the Leg piece. See this video for more information on this technique: https://youtu.be/paLzlAi--vk

5. SC, Inc, SC 3, starting in the last available stitch on the Body and finishing in the first available stitch on the Leg, work a Dec, working in the Leg only SC 3, starting in the last available stitch on the Leg and finishing in the first available stitch in the Body, work a Dec, SC in the same stitch that the last Dec ended in, <Dec>, SC, start a Dec in the same stitch as your last SC and complete the Dec in the first available stitch on the next Leg, working in the Leg only SC 3, starting in the last available stitch on the Leg and finishing in the first available stitch in the Body, work a Dec, SC 3, Inc, SC, Sl St to beginning stitch, Ch 1 [25]

> When you work into the Legs in this row, you will always be working as normal, inserting your hook from the outside/right side to the inside/wrong side of the Leg to complete the stitches. You will ignore all the stitches that were used to connect the Leg and the Body in the previous row.

6. SC, Dec, SC 7, Inc, SC 3, Inc, SC 7, Dec, SC, Sl St to beginning stitch, Ch 1 [25]

7. SC 25, Sl St to beginning stitch, Ch 1 [25]

8. SC, Dec, SC 19, Dec, SC, Sl St to beginning stitch, Ch 1 [23]

9. SC 23, Sl St to beginning stitch, Ch 1 [23]

10. SC 9, Dec, SC 4, Dec, SC 6, Sl St to beginning stitch, Ch 1 [21]

11. SC 5, Dec, SC 10, Dec, SC 2, Sl St to beginning stitch, Ch 1 [19]

12. Dec, SC 17, Sl St to beginning stitch, Ch 1 [18]

13. (SC 2, Dec, SC 2) x 3, Sl St to beginning stitch, Ch 1 [15]

14. (SC 3, Dec) x 3, Sl St to beginning stitch, Ch 1 [12]

15. SC 2, SC in the first stitch on Arm #1 and the first available stitch on the Body, SC in the next available stitch on the Arm and the next available stitch on the Body—working in the Body only—SC, Dec, SC, Dec, SC, SC in the first stitch on Arm #2 and the same stitch you worked the last SC stitch into on the Body, SC in the next available stitch on the Arm and the last available stitch on the Body, continue in spiral, DO NOT Sl St, Ch 1 [11]

When you work on a sitting Impkin, the way that you stuff the piece will affect the stability of its sitting position. Do not overstuff the Legs. As you stuff the feet and Body, pay attention to the sitting position to ensure that it sits flat on a flat surface. The first picture is incorrectly stuffed; the second picture is correctly stuffed.

You can optionally use glass gems to lend some weight in the bottom of the Body to provide added stability to the Impkin. Begin to stuff the Body medium-firm with fiberfill stuffing. Continue to stuff as you go. If you are going to use a hat of some kind, or if you want the head to be well supported, leave some room in the Body to insert a wire. For this project, I recommend a 0.3 in/0.75 cm diameter foam flexible curling rod. It is wired on the inside, and you can insert it into the neck of the Impkin. This rod will support the head under the weight of a hat, and the foam will protect the crochet work from the wire.

When you work into the Arm piece, insert your hook into the wrong side/inside of the Arm first, then insert your hook into the right side/outside of the Body next, and complete a SC through both at the same time. Do not work into the Sl St join from the Arms.

16. SC 2, starting in the first available stitch on the Arm, SC 3 around the outer edge of Arm #1—ignoring the stitches you used to attach the Arm—Dec, SC, Dec, SC 3 around the outer edge of Arm #2—ignoring the stitches you used to attach the Arm [11]

17. Dec, SC, Dec, Triple SC Dec, Dec, SC [6]

18. FLO [Inc x 6] [12]
19. (SC, Inc) x 6 [18]

20. (SC, Inc, SC) x 6 [24]
21. (SC 3, Inc) x 6 [30]
22. (SC 2, Inc, SC 2) x 6 [36]
23. SC 36 [36]

24. SC 36 [36]

25. SC 36 [36]
26. SC 16, (Dec, SC, Dec, SC, Dec) x 2, SC 4 [30]
27. SC 30 [30]
28. SC 30 [30]
29. SC 30 [30]
30. (SC 4, Dec) x 5 [25]

Insert 12 mm or 15 mm black safety eyes OR 18 mm or 23 mm colored iris safety eyes at the front of the face just above the decreases you worked in Rows 26 (or 1 row above that) with 3 or 4 stitch spaces between the eye posts. (The post will be inserted in a stitch space [a space between two stitch posts], and then you count 3–4 stitch spaces away from the post, and insert the next eye post into the next available stitch space.) Insert the eyes and then check to see if you like the placement before fastening them in place; adjust as necessary. If you are using a foam curling rod and/or wire, you can insert it at this point.

31. (SC 3, Dec) x 5 [20]
32. (SC, Dec, SC) x 5 [15]
33. (SC, Dec) x 5 [10]
34. Dec x 5 [5]

Fasten off with 12 in/30.5 cm yarn tail. Use the yarn tail to sew shut the hole in the top of the head. Weave in ends.

ANTENNAE

Impkin antennae may require some adjustment on your part to properly tune into the right radio station—just take your time and slowly turn them about until you pick something up. But once attuned properly to music the Impkin enjoys, the antennae can transform the Impkin into an impromptu stereo . . . though no antennae guarantee the Impkin a good singing voice. Other antennae can pick up emotions, new spectra of color, incoming weather, or even the presence of other Impkins or Stitchlings. Help your Impkin discover whatever they can detect!

ANTENNAE OPTIONS

Antennae Style 1

Antennae Style 3

Antennae Style 2

Antennae Style 4

ANTENNAE STYLE 1 (MAKE 2)

Any Color Yarn:
Approximately 13 yd/12 m total

1. SC 5 in Magic Circle, Sl St to beginning stitch, Ch 1 [5]
2. SC 2, Inc, SC 2, Sl St to beginning stitch, Ch 1 [6]
3. SC 2, Dec, SC 2, Sl St to beginning stitch, Ch 1 [5]
4. SC 5, Sl St to beginning stitch, Ch 1 [5]
5. SC 3, Dec, Sl St to beginning stitch, Ch 1 [4]
6–8. (3 rows of) SC 4, Sl St to beginning stitch, Ch 1 [4]
9. SC 3, Inc, Sl St to beginning stitch, Ch 1 [5]
10. SC 5, Sl St to beginning stitch, Ch 1 [5]
11. SC 2, Inc, SC 2, Sl St to beginning stitch, Ch 1 [6]
12. SC 6, Sl St to beginning stitch, Ch 1 [6]
13. (SC 2, Inc) x 2, Sl St to beginning stitch, Ch 1 [8]
14. (Inc, SC 3) x 2, Sl St to beginning stitch, Ch 1 [10]
15. (SC 2, Inc, SC 2) x 2, Sl St to beginning stitch [12]

Fasten off with 12 in/30.5 cm yarn tail.

Assembly

Pin in place on the head of the Impkin. You do not have to stuff with fiberfill at all. Sew to attach using yarn tails, and weave in ends.

ANTENNAE STYLE 2 (MAKE 2)

Any Color Yarn:
Approximately 6 yd/5.5 m total

1. Starting with a long enough yarn tail to weave in, Ch 13. Starting in the second Ch from hook, SC, HDC, SC 10, Ch 1, Turn [12]
2. Sl St 10, SC, HDC & SC, continue to crochet back down the OC side of Row 1, SC & HDC, SC, Sl St 10 [26]

Fasten off with 12 in/30.5 cm yarn tail.

Assembly

1. Pin in place on either side of the top of the head. Use the yarn tails to sew to attach, and weave in ends.
2. It may take some effort to tilt/bend the antenna so that your Impkin can pick up radio signals to a station that is playing music they enjoy. Be patient; you can do this.

Standing Body
Style 1, Arm Style 1,
Antennae Style 1

Standing Body
Style 1, Arm Style 1,
Antennae Style 2,
Pocket Belly,
Long, Droopy Ears

ANTENNAE STYLE 3 (MAKE 2)

Any Color Yarn:
Approximately 10 yd/9.25 m total

1. SC 6 in Magic Circle, Sl St to beginning stitch, Ch 1 [6]

2. (SC, Inc) x 3, Sl St to beginning stitch, Ch 1 [9]

3. SC 9, Sl St to beginning stitch, Ch 1 [9]

4. (SC, Dec) x 3, Sl St to beginning stitch, Ch 1 [6]

5-9. (5 rows of) SC 6, Sl St to beginning stitch, Ch 1

Fasten off with 12 in/30.5 cm yarn tail.

Assembly

Pin in place on either side of the top of the head. Use the yarn tails to sew to attach, and weave in ends.

ANTENNAE STYLE 4 (MAKE 2 OR MORE)

Any Color Yarn:
Approximately 6 yd/5.5 m total

1. Starting with a long enough yarn tail to weave in later, Ch 11. Starting in the second Ch from hook, SC 10, Ch 1, Turn [10]

2. (Sl St 2, Ch 2, Sl St in the second Ch from hook) x 5, Sl St in the same stitch that you last slip stitched into on the Antennae; now you will continue to work back down the Ch side of Row 1's stitches, Sl St into the next available stitch, Ch 2, Sl St in the second Ch from hook, Sl St in the same stitch that you last slip stitched into on the Antennae, Sl St, (Ch 2, Sl St in the second Ch from hook, Sl St 2) x 4 [22 (32 with picot stitches included)]

The "Ch 2, Sl St in the second Ch from hook" instruction is used to create a picot or a little decorative point along the edges of the Antennae.

Fasten off with 12 in/30.5 cm yarn tail.

Assembly

Pin in place on either side of the top of the head, use the yarn tails to sew to attach, and weave in ends.

Standing
Body Style 2,
Arm Style 2,
Antennae Style 4,
Dinosaur/Dragon
Tail, Belly Style 1

BELLY STYLES

*Give your Impkin its own look with a
unique belly style. There are four options:
a panel, a pocket, a ribbed style, or a
skeleton-like rib cage.*

BELLY OPTIONS

Panel Belly

Pocket Belly

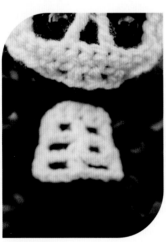

Rib Cage

Ribbed Belly

PANEL BELLY

Any Color Yarn:
Approximately 5 yd/4.5 m total

1. Ch 5, Turn, starting in the second Ch from hook, Inc, SC 2, HDC 5 in the last Ch stitch, continue to crochet back along the OC, SC 2, Inc, Sl St to beginning stitch, Ch 1 [13]

2. SC, Inc, SC 2, HDC Inc x 5, SC 3, Inc, Sl St to beginning stitch, Ch 1 [20]

3. SC, Inc, SC 3, (HDC, HDC Inc) x 5, SC 3, Inc, SC, Sl St to beginning stitch [27]

Fasten off with 24 in/61 cm yarn tail.

Assembly

Pin to attach over the belly of the Impkin. Use yarn tails to sew around the edge of the belly piece, and weave in ends.

POCKET BELLY

Any Color Yarn:
Approximately 6 yd/5.5 m total

1. Starting with a long enough yarn tail to weave in later, SC 5 in Magic Circle, Ch 1, Turn, tighten the Magic Circle [5]

2. Inc x 2, SC, Inc x 2, Ch 1, Turn [9]

3. (SC, Inc) x 2, SC, (Inc, SC) x 2, Ch 1, Turn [13]

4. (SC, Inc, SC) x 2, SC, (SC, Inc, SC) x 2, Ch 1, Turn [17]

5. (SC 3, Inc) x 2, SC, (Inc, SC 3) x 2, Ch 1, reorient to work across the unfinished straight edge [21]

6. Starting by working around the side of the last stitch of Row 5, SC about 11 stitches across the edge (it is okay if this is not exact, but it should take about 11 to get across the straight edge) [11]

Fasten off with 18 in/45.75 cm yarn tail.

Assembly

1. Pin to attach the piece on the belly. Once you are satisfied with placement, sew around the curved outer edge of the piece created by Row 5. Do not sew along the straight edge created by Row 6; leave this open to create a pocket. Weave in ends.

2. Put something special and secret inside the pocket. Like a shiny penny. Or a button. Or the One Ring.

Standing
Body Style 2,
Arm Style 2,
Pocket Belly,
Elf Ears, Medium
Wavy Horns

WHEN IMPKINS GET TOGETHER, IT ALMOST INEVITABLY
LEADS TO MUTUAL ADMIRATION OF STYLE, COLOR, DESIGN,
AND ORNAMENTATION. AND THEN, WHEN THEY RETURN TO
THEIR CRAFTERS, THEY MIGHT BEG OR PLEAD FOR SOME
NEW FEATURE THEY DISCOVERED IN A FRIEND. BE WARY OF
GRANTING YOUR IMPKIN'S EVERY WHIM, LEST THEY NEVER LET
YOU REST . . . BUT AN OCCASIONAL TREAT NEVER HURTS!

– Notes from the field, L. Mossgrove

RIB CAGE

White Yarn:
Approximately 3 yd/2.75 m total

1. Starting with a long enough yarn tail to weave in later, Ch 6, Turn, starting in the second Ch from hook, SC 5, Ch 2, Turn [5]

> The Ch 2 instruction at the end of this row is a turning chain. Do not crochet into it.

2. HDC, Ch 2, Skip 1 stitch, HDC, Ch 2, Skip 1 stitch, HDC, Ch 2, Turn [3]

> The Ch 2 instruction at the end of this row is a turning chain. Do not crochet into it.

3. HDC, Ch 3, Skip the Ch-2 Space, HDC, Ch 3, Skip the Ch-2 Space, HDC, Ch 2, Turn [3]

> The Ch 2 instruction at the end of this row is a turning chain. Do not crochet into it.

4. HDC, Ch 3, Skip the Ch-3 Space, HDC, Ch 3, Skip the Ch-3 Space, HDC [3]

Fasten off with 24 in/61 cm yarn tail.

Assembly

Pin to attach to the chest area of the Impkin. Sew to attach, and weave in ends. You only need to sew around the outer edge of the ribs and tack down the center as needed; it is not necessary to sew down each "rib."

Standing Body Style 2, Arm Style 2, Rib Cage, Skull Mask

RIBBED BELLY

Belly Color Yarn:
Approximately 7 yd/6.5 m total

1. Starting with a long enough yarn tail to weave in later, Ch 4, Turn, starting in the second Ch from hook, SC, Inc, SC, Ch 1, Turn [4]

2. BLO [Inc, SC 2, Inc], Ch 1, Turn [6]

3. BLO [SC 6], Ch 1, Turn [6]

4. BLO [SC, Inc, SC 2, Inc, SC], Ch 1, Turn [8]

5-9. (5 rows of) BLO [SC 8], Ch 1, Turn [8]

10. BLO [SC, Dec, SC 2, Dec, SC], Ch 1, Turn [6]

11. BLO [Dec, SC 2, Dec], Do not Ch 1, Do not Turn [4]

12. Work a SC in the same stitch that the last Dec of Row 11 ended in, SC about 9 stitches along the unfinished edge of the piece toward the OC, Inc in the OC, continue to crochet across the chain side of Row 1, SC, Inc, SC about 10 stitches along the unfinished edge of the piece toward the start of Row 11, Sl St into the first Dec from Row 11 [~26]

Fasten off with 18 in/45.75 cm yarn tail.

Assembly

Pin to attach over the belly of the Impkin. Use yarn tails to sew around the edge of the belly piece and weave in ends.

I HAVE HEARD REPORTS THAT SOME CONSIDER RUBBING AN IMPKIN'S TUMMY A GOOD LUCK RITUAL. SUPERSTITIOUS POPPYCOCK, I SAY. RUBBING AN IMPKIN'S TUMMY IS A GOOD WAY TO MAKE IT PURR, AND THAT IS REWARD ENOUGH.

– Notes from the field, L. Mossgrove

EARS

Impkins seem to express a lot of individuality with their ears! Eleven different types have been spotted in the wild, but it seems likely there are many yet to be discovered.

EAR OPTIONS

Round, Folded Ears

Fin Ears

Large, Round Ears

Long, Droopy Ears

Elf Ears

Puppy Dog Ears

Cat Ears

Small, Round Ears

Pony Ears

Spiky Ears

Funnel Ears

ROUND, FOLDED EARS (MAKE 2)

Any Color Yarn:
Approximately 10 yd/9.25 m total

1. Starting with a long enough yarn tail to weave in later, SC 6 in Magic Circle, Sl St to beginning stitch, Ch 1 [6]

2. Inc x 5, Ch 1, Turn [10]

3. SC, HDC Inc, (HDC, HDC Inc) x 3, HDC, Inc, Ch 1, Turn [15]

4. Inc, HDC 2, (HDC 2, HDC Inc) x 3, HDC 2, Inc [20]

Fasten off with 12 in/30.5 cm yarn tail.

Assembly

Fold in half and pin in place on the head. Once you are pleased with placement, sew to attach using yarn tails. Weave in ends.

Be forewarned: Merely attaching ears does not mean your Impkin will listen to you!

LONG, DROOPY EARS (MAKE 2)

Any Color Yarn:
Approximately 5 yd/4.5 m total

1. Starting with a long enough yarn tail to weave in later, Ch 11, starting in the second Ch from hook, HDC, DC 2, HDC 3, SC 4, Ch 1, Turn [10]

2. SC 9, Inc, continue to crochet around to the other side of the stitches in Row 1, Inc, SC 9, Ch 1, Turn [22]

3. SC 5, HDC 4, HDC & DC, Triple DC Inc, Triple DC Inc, DC & HDC, HDC 4, SC 5, Ch 1 [28]

4. Fold the ear so that the top, short, flat edge of the ear is folded in half, and then work SC 2 across the folded edge to fasten it together [2]

Fasten off with 12 in/30.5 cm yarn tail.

Assembly

Pin in place on the head. Once you are pleased with placement, sew to attach using yarn tails and weave in ends.

Standing Body
Style 1,
Arm Style 1,
Round, Folded
Ears

Standing Body Style 1, Arm Style 1, Long, Droopy Ears, Wide and Curled Horns, Short Vest

CAT EARS (MAKE 2)

Inner Ear Color Yarn: Approximately 5 yd/4.5 m total

Body Color Yarn for Outer Ear: Approximately 9 yd/8.25 m total

Part 1: Inner Ear Color Yarn

1. In Magic Circle, SC 3, Ch 1, Turn, tighten the Magic Circle [3]
2. SC, Inc, SC, Ch 1, Turn [4]
3. SC, Inc x 2, SC, Ch 1, Turn [6]
4. SC 2, Inc x 2, SC 2, Ch 1, Turn [8]
5. SC 2, Inc, SC 2, Inc, SC 2 [10]

Fasten off with 12 in/30.5 cm yarn tail.

Part 2: Body Color Yarn

1. In Magic Circle, SC 3, Ch 1, Turn, tighten the Magic Circle [3]
2. SC, Inc, SC, Ch 1, Turn [4]
3. SC, Inc x 2, SC, Ch 1, Turn [6]
4. SC 2, Inc x 2, SC 2, Ch 1, Turn [8]
5. SC 2, Inc, SC 2, Inc, SC 2, Ch 1, Turn to work back up the edge toward the Magic Circle/Row 1 [10]

6. Hold Part 1 in front of Part 2, working through both pieces at the same time, SC 5 up one side to the point, Triple SC Inc in the topmost Magic Circle stitch, SC 5 down the other side [13]

Fasten off with 12 in/30.5 cm yarn tail.

Assembly

Curve the bottom of the ear as you pin to attach to the head (as shown in the photos). Once you are satisfied with placement, sew to attach using yarn tails and weave in ends.

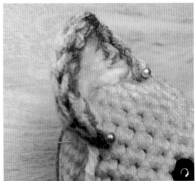

If you opt for earrings, be sure to make time to have a serious conversation with your Impkin about the fact that earrings are decoration and NOT food.

Standing Body
Style 1,
Arm Style 1,
Panel Belly,
Cat Ears

Standing Body
Style 1,
Arm Style 1,
Fin Ears, Triangle
Scales, Dinosaur/
Dragon Tail

BE SURE TO TALK TO YOUR IMPKINS ABOUT WHAT MAKES THEM SPECIAL AND WHAT MAKES THEM IMPKINS. SOME IMPKINS GIVEN HORNS HAVE THOUGHT THEY WERE UNICORNS; OTHERS GIVEN WINGS OR SCALES OR WEBBED EARS HAVE THOUGHT THEMSELVES DRAGONS. YOU DON'T WANT YOUR IMPKINS TO BELIEVE THEY ARE DRAGONS WITH SUCH VERVE THAT THEY BEGIN TO BREATHE FLAME!

– Notes from the field, L. Mossgrove

FIN EARS (MAKE 2)

Body Color Yarn:
Approximately 7 yd/6.5 m total

Accent Color Yarn:
Approximately 9 yd/8.25 m total

Part 1: Body Color Yarn

1. Starting with a long enough yarn tail to weave in later, Ch 5, Turn, starting in the second Ch from hook, SC 4, Ch 1, Turn [4]

> The right side of Row 1 will be on the wrong side of the work when the ear is complete.

2. BLO [SC, HDC, DC, Half Trip], Ch 1, Turn [4]
3. BLO [SC 4], Ch 1, Turn [4]
4. BLO [SC, HDC, DC, Half Trip], Ch 1, Turn [4]
5. BLO [SC 4], Ch 1, Turn [4]
6. BLO [SC, HDC, DC, Half Trip], Ch 1, Turn [4]
7. BLO [SC 4], Ch 1, Turn [4]
8. BLO [SC, HDC, DC, Half Trip], Ch 1, Turn [4]
9. BLO [Sl St 4] [4]

Fasten off with 18 in/45.75 cm yarn tail.

The wrong side has 4 BLO ridges and 2 edges. The right side has 3 BLO ridges and 2 edges.

Wrong side of the work

Right side of the work

Part 2: Accent Color Yarn

1. Attach the yarn around the final Sl St of Row 9 in Part 1, working along the edge created in Row 9, SC 3, Inc, Ch 2, Turn [5]

2. Starting in the second Ch from hook, Sl St 6, Ch 1, make 1 Dec along the unfinished (inner) edge between the Accent Row just made and the next available BLO ridge on the right side of the work [7]

3. Working along the next available BLO ridge, SC 3, Inc, Ch 2, Turn [5]

Make sure you are working along the ridge on the RIGHT SIDE of your work. You may need to fold the work so that the ridge is at the top of the fold to make it easier to work into.

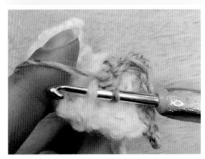

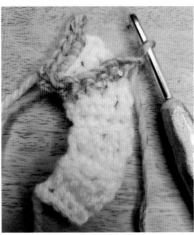

4. Starting in the second Ch from hook, Sl St 6, Ch 1, make 1 Dec along the unfinished (inner) edge between the Accent Row just made and the next available BLO ridge on the right side of the work [7]

5. Working along the next available BLO ridge, SC 3, Inc, Ch 2, Turn [5]

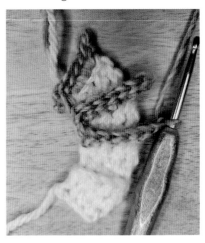

6. Starting in the second Ch from hook, Sl St 6, Ch 1, make 1 Dec along the unfinished (inner) edge between the Accent Row just made and the next available BLO ridge on the right side of the work [7]

7. Working along the next available BLO ridge, SC 3, Inc, Ch 2, Turn [5]

8. Starting in the second Ch from hook, Sl St 6, Ch 1, make 1 Dec along the unfinished (inner) edge between the Accent Row just made and the next available BLO ridge on the right side of the work [7]

9. Working along the next available final edge of the ear, SC 3, Inc, Ch 2, Turn [5]

10. Starting in the second Ch from hook, Sl St 6 [6]

Fasten off with 18 in/45.75 cm yarn tail.

Assembly

Pin both ears to attach to either side of the Impkin's head. Sew to attach using yarn tails and weave in ends.

Standing Body
Style 1,
Arm Style 1, Fin Ears,
Triangle Scales,
Dinosaur/Dragon Tail

ELF EARS (MAKE 2)

Body Color Yarn:
Approximately 12 yd/11 m total

1. Starting with a long enough yarn tail to weave in, Ch 13, Turn, starting in the second Ch from hook, Dec, SC 10, Ch 1, Turn [11]

2. SC 9, Dec, Ch 1, Turn [10]

3. Dec, SC 8, Ch 1, Turn [9]

4. SC 7, Dec, Ch 1, Turn [8]

5. Dec, SC 6, Ch 1, Turn [7]

6. Dec, SC 3, Dec, Ch 1, Turn [5]

7. Dec, SC, Dec, Ch 1, Turn [3]

8. Triple SC Dec, SC in the same stitch that the Triple SC Dec ended in, continuing to crochet in that direction along the unfinished edge of the ear toward the point, SC about 8 to the point, work a Triple SC Inc in the corner tip, and then Sl St 11 back along the straight edge of Row 1 to the OC

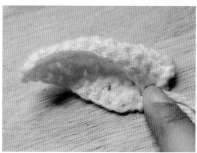

Fasten off with 12 in/30.5 cm yarn tail.

Assembly

Fold the top long, flat edge over itself to create a fold in the ear. Pin to attach to the head. Once you are satisfied with placement, sew to attach and weave in ends.

MANY IMPKINS ARE OBSESSED WITH THE PANOPLY OF ALL THINGS BRIGHT AND BEAUTIFUL IN THE WORLD. THEY WILL OFTEN SEEK OUT NEW BITS OF COLOR AND LIFE. ALL THE BETTER IF THE COLOR THEY FIND MATCHES OR COMPLEMENTS THEIR OWN . . . AND IN THE BEST CASES, THE COLOR CAN EASILY BE TURNED INTO SOME NEW ORNAMENT OR ADORNMENT! YOU WOULD DO WELL TO KEEP AROUND SOME BITS OF COLOR TO EITHER MATCH OR COMPLEMENT YOUR IMPKIN, JUST IN CASE THEY WANT TO ADD SOMETHING TO THEIR ATTIRE.

– Notes from the field, L. Mossgrove

Sitting Body
Style 2,
Arm Style 2,
Spiky Ears,
Backpack

SPIKY EARS (MAKE 2)

Body Color Yarn:
Approximately 11 yd/10 m total

1. Starting with a long enough yarn tail to weave in, SC 6 in Magic Circle, Sl St to beginning stitch, Ch 1 [6]
2. Inc x 5, Ch 1, Turn [10]
3. SC 2, (SC, Inc) x 3, SC 2, Turn [13]

4. Ch 4, starting in the second Ch from hook, SC 3, Skip the first available stitch on the Ear from Row 3, Sl St into the next available stitch, Sl St, (Ch 4, starting in the second Ch from hook, SC 3, Sl St 2) x 3, Sl St 4 [24]

Fasten off with 12 in/30.5 cm yarn tail.

Assembly

Fold the top flat edge over itself to create a fold in the ear. Pin to attach to the head. Once you are satisfied with placement, sew to attach and weave in ends.

SMALL, ROUND EARS (MAKE 2)

Body Color Yarn: Approximately 5 yd/4.5 m total

1. Starting with a long enough yarn tail to weave in, SC 6 in Magic Circle, Sl St to beginning stitch, Ch 1 [6]
2. Inc x 5, Ch 1, Turn [10]
3. SC 10 [10]

Fasten off with 12 in/30.5 cm yarn tail.

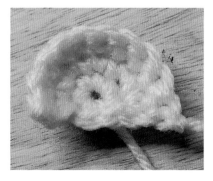

Assembly

Pin the ear in place on the head. Once you are satisfied with placement, sew to attach and weave in ends.

Standing Body
Style 2,
Arm Style 1,
Small, Round Ears

Sitting Body
Style 1,
Arm Style 1,
Large, Round Ears,
Rounded Scales

LARGE, ROUND EARS (MAKE 2)

Body Color Yarn: Approximately 8 yd/7.25 m total

1. Starting with a long enough yarn tail to weave in, SC 6 in Magic Circle, Sl St to beginning stitch, Ch 1 [6]
2. Inc x 6, Sl St to beginning stitch, Ch 1 [12]
3. (SC, Inc) x 6, Sl St to beginning stitch, Ch 1 [18]
4. HDC 2, Inc, (SC 2, Inc) x 3, SC, HDC, HDC Inc [20]

Fasten off with 12 in/30.5 cm yarn tail.

Assembly

Fold the side of the ear over on itself slightly to create a left ear and a right ear. Pin the ears in place on the head. Once you are satisfied with placement, sew to attach and weave in ends.

PUPPY DOG EARS (MAKE 2)

Body Color Yarn: Approximately 10 yd/9.25 m total

1. Starting with a long enough yarn tail to weave in later, SC 2 in Magic Circle, tighten the circle, Ch 1, Turn [2]
2. SC, <Dec>, SC, Ch 1, Turn [3]
3. SC, Inc, SC, Ch 1, Turn [4]
4. SC 2, <Dec>, SC 2, Ch 1, Turn [5]
5. SC 2, Inc, SC 2, Ch 1, Turn [6]
6-9. (4 rows of) SC 6, Ch 1, Turn [6]

10. Dec, SC 2, Dec, Ch 1, reorient so that you will crochet down the unfinished edge toward the Magic Circle when working the next row [4]

11. Start by working around the side of the last stitch you made in Row 10, SC 10, Triple SC Inc in the Original Magic Circle, SC 10 [23]

Fasten off with 12 in/30.5 cm yarn tail.

Assembly

Pin the ears in place on the head. Once you are satisfied with placement, sew to attach and weave in ends.

PONY EARS (MAKE 2)

Body Color Yarn: Approximately 7 yd/6.5 m total

1. Starting with a long enough yarn tail to weave in later, Ch 2, Turn, starting in the second Ch from hook, Inc, Ch 1, Turn [2]
2. SC, <Dec>, SC, Ch 1, Turn [3]
3. SC, Inc, SC, Ch 1, Turn [4]
4. SC 2, <Dec>, SC 2, Ch 1, Turn [5]
5. SC 2, Inc, SC 2, Ch 1, reorient so that you will be working up the unfinished edge of the work toward Row 1 [6]

6. Start by working around the side of the last stitch you made in Row 5, SC 5, working into the OC, SC & HDC & SC (this is the tip of the ear), SC 5 down the other side [13]

Fasten off with 12 in/30.5 cm yarn tail.

Assembly

Pin the ears in place on the head. Once you are satisfied with placement, sew to attach and weave in ends.

FUNNEL EARS (MAKE 2)

Body Color Yarn: Approximately 14 yd/12.75 m total

1. Starting with 12 in/30.5 cm yarn tail, Ch 15, Sl St to the beginning Ch to make a circle of chain stitches, Ch 1 [15]

2. Working around the chain stitch circle you created in Row 1, SC 18, Sl St to beginning stitch, Ch 1 [18]

> When you work the SC stitches around the chain stitch circle, you will not work into the individual chain stitches; instead, you will encase the chain stitches in the SC stitches you make.

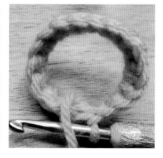

3. (SC 2, Dec, SC 2) x 3, Sl St to beginning stitch, Ch 1 [15]
4. (SC 3, Dec) x 3, Sl St to beginning stitch, Ch 1 [12]
5. (SC, Dec, SC) x 3, Sl St to beginning stitch, Ch 1 [9]
6–8. (3 rows of) SC 9, Sl St to beginning stitch, Ch 1 [9]

9. SC 9, Sl St to beginning stitch [9]

Fasten off with 12 in/30.5 cm yarn tail.

Assembly

Pin the ears in place on the head. Once you are satisfied with placement, sew to attach and weave in ends.

FACE STYLES

*From masks to a beard, snoot, eye patch,
and more, there are several facial features
that can add personality to your Impkin.*

IMPKINS ARE VARIED, JUST LIKE PEOPLE; WHERE
SOME IMPKINS ARE PARAGONS OF MODERATION
AND RESTRAINT, OTHERS HAVE A TENDENCY TO
WANT ALL THE THINGS. IF YOUR IMPKIN STARTS
ASKING FOR A MASK, BEARD, SNOOT, EYE PATCH,
AND TENTACLES ALL AT ONCE, TRY GIVING THEM
ONE FEATURE AT A TIME UNTIL THEY'RE SATISFIED.

– Notes from the field, L. Mossgrove

FACE OPTIONS

Skull Mask

Ninja Mask

Beard

Snoot

Eye Patch

Face Tentacles

SKULL MASK

White Yarn:
Approximately 8 yd/7.25 m total

1. Starting with a long enough yarn tail to weave in later, Ch 15, Turn, starting in the second Ch from hook, SC 14, Ch 2, Turn [14]

> The Ch 2 at the end of this row is a turning chain only; do not crochet into it.

2. DC, Half Trip, Ch 4, Skip 3 stitches, Half Trip, Skip 2 stitches, Half Trip, Ch 4, Skip 3 stitches, Half Trip, DC, Ch 1, Turn [6]
3. Dec, SC 5 around the next Ch space, Dec, SC 5 around the next Ch space, Dec, Ch 1, Turn [13]
4. Dec, SC 9, Dec, Ch 1, Turn [11]
5. Dec, SC 7, Dec, Ch 1, Turn [9]

6. Dec, SC 5, Dec & SC, continue to crochet along the unfinished edge toward the OC, SC 5, Triple SC Inc in the corner, continue to crochet along the OC, Sl St 3, Ch 2, working in the next available stitch HDC, Ch 1, Skip 1 stitch, HDC, Ch 1, HDC, Ch 1, Skip 1 stitch, HDC, Ch 2, Sl St 3, Triple SC Inc in the corner, continue to crochet along the unfinished edge back toward the beginning of this row, SC 5, SC in the same stitch as the first stitch you started working into for the first Dec of this row, Sl St to beginning stitch [35]

Fasten off with 24 in/61 cm yarn tail.

Assembly

Pin to attach to the face of the Impkin, centering the safety eyes in the eyeholes of the skull piece. Sew to attach using yarn tails and weave in ends.

NINJA MASK

Any Color Yarn:
Approximately 19 yd/17.25 m total

1. Starting with a long enough yarn tail to weave in later, Ch 81, Turn, starting in the second Ch from hook, SC 80, Ch 1, Turn [80]
2. Dec, SC 33, Ch 3, skip 3 stitches, HDC 4, Ch 3, skip 3 stitches, SC 33, Dec, Ch 1, Turn [78]

> In this row, the chain stitches are included in the stitch count and you will crochet into them in the next row.

3. Dec, SC 74, Dec [76]

Fasten off with 12 in/30.5 cm yarn tail.

Assembly

Pin to attach to the face of the Impkin, with the eyeholes centered over the Impkin's eyes. You can weave the ends into the mask itself and tie it in a knot at the back of the head, for a removable mask, or you can sew it to attach it to the head of the Impkin and tie it in place, for a permanent mask.

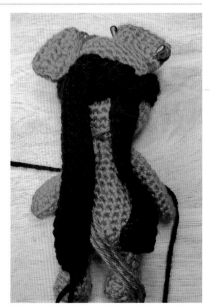

Standing Body
Style 2,
Arm Style 2,
Ninja Mask

BEARD

Any Color Yarn:
Approximately 6 yd/5.5 m total

1. Start with a long enough yarn tail to weave in later, Ch 4, starting in the second Ch from hook, SC, Small Bobble, SC, Ch 1, Turn [3]

> A Small Bobble is worked as follows: YO, insert your hook into the next available stitch, YO, pull up, YO, insert your hook into the same stitch, YO, pull up, YO, pull through all remaining loops.

2. SC & Small Bobble, SC, Small Bobble & SC, Ch 1, Turn [5]

3. Small Bobble, SC, Small Bobble, SC, Small Bobble, Ch 1, Turn [5]

4. SC, Small Bobble & SC, SC, SC & Small Bobble, SC, Ch 1, Turn [7]

5. (Small Bobble, SC) x 3, Small Bobble, Ch 1, Turn [7]

6. SC, Small Bobble & SC, SC, Small Bobble, SC, SC & Small Bobble, SC, Ch 1, Turn [9]

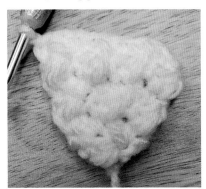

7. (Small Bobble, SC) x 4, Small Bobble, Ch 1, Turn [9]

8. SC, Small Bobble, Ch 5, Skip 5 stitches, Small Bobble, SC [4]

Fasten off with 12 in/30.5 cm yarn tail.

Assembly

Pin to attach to the face of the Impkin. Once you are satisfied with placement, sew to attach and weave in ends.

Standing Body
Style 2,
Arm Style 2, Beard,
Viking Hat

IN SOME CASES, THE GRANDIOSITY OF AN IMPKIN'S FORM—THEIR HAT, THEIR CLOTHES, THEIR OTHER ADORNMENTS—CAN GIVE THEM A RATHER UNREALISTIC SENSE OF WHAT THEY SHOULD BE DOING AND HOW THEY SHOULD BE ACTING. KNOW THAT IF YOU OUTFIT AN IMPKIN IN THE ATTIRE OF A VIKING, YOU CAN'T JUST EXPECT THE IMPKIN TO SIT AROUND IDLY ALL DAY! VIKING IMPKINS ARE GOING TO SEEK OUT THE SEA, AND WHEN THEY FIND IT, THEY'RE GOING TO BUILD A LONGSHIP TO GO FIND NEW LANDS!

– Notes from the field, L. Mossgrove

SNOOT

Any Color Yarn:
Approximately 8 yd/7.25 m total

1. Starting with a long enough yarn tail to weave in later, Ch 8, Sl St to the beginning chain to make a circle of chain stitches, Ch 1 [8]
2. Working around the chain stitch circle you created in Row 1, SC 10, continue in spiral [10]

> When you work the SC stitches around the chain stitch circle, you will not work into the individual chain stitches; instead, you will encase the chain stitches in the SC stitches you make.

3. (SC 3, Dec) x 2 [8]
4. Inc, SC 2, 2 Dec in 3 SC, SC 2 [8]
5. SC 8 [8]
6. SC, Inc, SC 2, 2 Dec in 3 SC, SC [8]
7. SC 8 [8]
8. SC, Inc, SC 2, 2 Dec in 3 SC, SC [8]
9. SC 8 [8]
10. SC 2, Inc, SC 2, 2 Dec in 3 SC [8]
11. SC 8 [8]
12. SC 2, Inc, SC 2, 2 Dec in 3 SC [8]
13. SC 8 [8]
14. (SC, Inc) x 4 [12]
15. (SC, Inc, SC) x 4 [16]

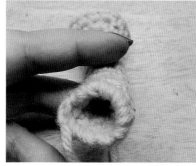

Fasten off with 12 in/30.5 cm yarn tail.

Assembly

Pin in place on the center of the face of the Impkin. Once satisfied with placement, use the yarn tail to sew to attach and weave in the ends.

AS YOU ARE WORKING ON YOUR IMPKIN, YOU MIGHT REALIZE THEY ARE TRYING TO LET YOU KNOW HOW MUCH THEY WOULD APPRECIATE A SNOOT. NOT EVERY IMPKIN NEEDS OR WANTS A SNOOT, BUT SOME CRAVE A SNOOT MORE THAN ANYTHING. BE SURE TO OBLIGE THEM WITH A REGAL AND MAJESTIC SNOOT, A REAL HONKER, THAT THEY CAN PROUDLY TOOT AND SNIFF THROUGH TO THEIR HEART'S CONTENT. AND DO NOT CONFUSE A NOSE WITH A SNOOT, OR EVEN A SNOUT! IMPKIN SNOOTS ARE A VERY PRECIOUS AND SPECIAL THING!

– Notes from the field, L. Mossgrove

EYE PATCH

Any Color Yarn:
Approximately 2 yd/1.75 m total

1. Starting with a long enough yarn tail to weave in later, Ch 31, starting in the second Ch from hook, HDC 3, Ch 1, Turn [3]

2. HDC 3 [3]

Fasten off with 12 in/30.5 cm yarn tail.

Assembly

Pin the widest part of the Eye Patch over the eye you want to cover. Pin the chain length so that it wraps around the head of the Impkin and back to the patch. Sew to attach to the head of the Impkin using the yarn tail and weave in ends.

Standing
Body Style 2,
Arm Style 2,
Eye Patch,
Puppy Dog Ears

SOME CRAFTERS FRET ABOUT WHAT TO GIVE THEIR IMPKIN. FLOPPY EARS OR STRAIGHT EARS? AN EYE PATCH OR THREE EYES? SNOOT OR NO SNOOT? THE TRUTH IS THAT IMPKINS ONLY EVER WANT TO EXIST EXACTLY AS THEY WERE MEANT TO, AND MORE THAN ANYTHING, CRAFTERS JUST NEED TO FOLLOW THEIR OWN IMAGINATIONS AND HEARTS TO CRAFT A HAPPY IMPKIN.

– Notes from the field, L. Mossgrove

Standing Body
Style 2,
Arm Style 2,
Face Tentacles,
Bat Wings

FACE TENTACLES

Any Color Yarn:
Approximately 20 yd/18.25 m
total

1. Starting with a long enough yarn tail to weave in later, Ch 21, starting in the second Ch from hook, Sl St, (SC 2, Inc) x 3, (HDC, HDC Inc) x 5, Ch 21, Turn [28]

2. Starting in the second Ch from hook, Sl St, (SC 2, Inc) x 3, (HDC, HDC Inc) x 5, Ch 21, Turn [28]

3. Starting in the second Ch from hook, Sl St, (SC 2, Inc) x 3, (HDC, HDC Inc) x 5, Ch 21, Turn [28]

4. Starting in the second Ch from hook, Sl St, (SC 2, Inc) x 3, (HDC, HDC Inc) x 5, Ch 21, Turn [28]

5. Starting in the second Ch from hook, Sl St, (SC 2, Inc) x 3, (HDC, HDC Inc) x 5, Ch 26, Turn [28]

NOTE: You chain 26 here, as this creates more length between what will be the back row of face tentacles and the front row of face tentacles. Rows 1 through 5 will be positioned directly against the Impkin's face, and Rows 6 through 9 will be pinned on top of Rows 1 through 5. The added chain length gives the flexibility necessary for correct positioning.

----

6. Starting in the second Ch from hook, Sl St, (SC 2, Inc) x 3, (HDC, HDC Inc) x 5, Ch 21, Turn [28]

7. Starting in the second Ch from hook, Sl St, (SC 2, Inc) x 3, (HDC, HDC Inc) x 5, Ch 21, Turn [28]

8. Starting in the second Ch from hook, Sl St, (SC 2, Inc) x 3, (HDC, HDC Inc) x 5, Ch 21, Turn [28]

9. Starting in the second Ch from hook, Sl St, (SC 2, Inc) x 3, (HDC, HDC Inc) x 5 [28]

Fasten off with 24 in/61 cm yarn tail.

Assembly

1. Pin the top straight edge of Rows 1 through 5 against the face of the Impkin just below the eye line.

2. Fold Rows 6 through 9 over the pinned Rows 1 to 5, and pin against the same line. Center each of the tentacles from Row 6 to Row 9 between each of the tentacles from Row 1 to Row 5.

3. Use the yarn tail to sew to attach along the top edge of the piece just below the eyes. Weave in the ends.

HATS AND HAIRSTYLES

Impkins adore fancy hats! Top hats, pointy wizard hats, pixie hoods, sparkling crowns, mushroom toppers . . . you name it, they'll wear it. And if they aren't wearing a hat, it's likely because they want to show off their colorful mohawk or flowing mane.

HAT AND HAIRSTYLE OPTIONS

Pixie Hood

Round Mushroom Cap

Curved Pointed Hat

Leaf Topper

Long, Curly Mane

Short-Pieced Mane/Mohawk

Pieced Lion's Mane

Top Hat

Flower Hat

Wide Crown

Small Crown

Smooth Wizard/
Witch Hat

Wrinkled Wizard/Witch Hat

Strawberry Stem Cap

Mandrake Topper

Viking Hat

Pumpkin Stem Cap

Hood and Cape

Pointed Mushroom Cap

Twisted Mushroom Cap

Feather Topper

PIXIE HOOD

Any Color Yarn:
Approximately 25 yd/22.75 m
total

1. Starting with a long enough yarn tail to weave in, Ch 29, Turn, starting in the second Ch from hook, SC 28, Ch 1, Turn [28]
2. SC 28, Ch 1, Turn [28]
3. SC 28, Ch 1, Turn [28]
4. SC 28, Ch 1, Turn [28]
5. SC 28, Ch 1, Turn [28]
6. SC 28, Ch 1, Turn [28]
7. SC 28, Ch 1, Turn [28]
8. SC 28, Ch 1, Turn [28]
9. SC 13, Inc x 2, SC 13, Ch 1, Turn [30]
10. SC 14, Inc x 2, SC 14, Ch 1, Turn [32]
11. SC 15, Inc x 2, SC 15, Ch 1, Turn [34]
12. SC 16, Inc x 2, SC 16, Ch 1, reorient to work back along the straight unfinished edge of the piece [36]

13. Triple SC Dec, Dec, Triple SC Dec, Dec, Triple SC Dec to the very corner edge, Ch 31, Turn [5]

> The chain stitches at the end of Rows 13 and 14 and the subsequent stitches at the beginning of Rows 14 and 15 make little drawstrings for the Pixie Hood. You can adjust the length to suit your Impkin's preference (Ch 61 for a more dramatic bow or Ch 15 for just two little curled strings).
>
> If you would like your Pixie Hood without strings, skip the chain and turn, and proceed with the Sl St 28 back along Row 1 instructions in Row 14.

14. Starting in the second Ch from hook, SC & HDC & HDC, Sl St 29 (OR 59 OR 13) back along the chain stitches, Sl St 28 back along Row 1/the front of the work, Ch 31 (OR 61, OR 15), Turn [60 (OR 90 OR 44)]

> If you would like your Pixie Hood without strings, skip the chain and turn, and proceed with the Triple SC Dec, Dec, etc., instruction in Row 15.

15. Starting in the second Ch from hook, SC & HDC & HDC, Sl St 29 (OR 59, OR 13) back along the chain stitches, working along the straight unfinished edge of the piece, Triple SC Dec, Dec, Triple SC Dec, Dec, Triple SC Dec, Ch 1 [37 (OR 67 OR 21)]

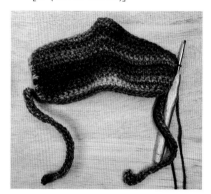

THE COLD DOESN'T MUCH AFFECT IMPKINS, NOR DOES THE SUN CAUSE THEM TO SQUINT OR SWEAT. THE HATS THEY DESIRE AND WEAR ARE PURELY DECORATIVE . . . WHICH IS TO SAY, THEY ARE A MATTER OF SOME PRIDE AND IMPORT FOR THE IMPKIN. A GOOD HAT FROM YOUR CRAFTER CAN BE THE PERFECT BOON TO AN IMPKIN'S CONFIDENCE. NEVER UNDERESTIMATE THE POWER OF YOUR HATTERY!

– Notes from the field, L. Mossgrove

16. Fold the hat in half so that Row 12 is folded in half and pressed against itself, working through both sides of Row 12 at the same time, work up to the point/tip of the hat, SC 18 [18]

You can fasten off here with a long enough yarn tail to weave in, or you can Ch 1, Turn, and Sl St back down the SC stitches you made in Row 16 and then fasten off with a yarn tail long enough to weave in.

Assembly

When you place this hat on the head of an Impkin, you can simply tie it in place and make it easy to put on and take off in the future, or you can sew it in place using yarn tails. You can also put a small amount of stuffing up in the point of the hat to fill it out before placing it on the head of the Impkin.

ROUND MUSHROOM CAP

Underside Mushroom Cap Color Yarn: Approximately 25 yd/22.75 m total

Mushroom Cap Color Yarn: Approximately 45 yd/41.25 m total

> This particular hat style is heavy. If you do not reinforce the neck of the Impkin with some kind of wire, dowel, or the like, the head will be too heavy to be supported by the neck. But if you're okay with a floppy/droopy-headed Impkin, that's fine.

Part 1: Underside Mushroom Cap Color Yarn

1. SC 6 in Magic Circle, Sl St to beginning stitch, Ch 1 [6]

2. Inc x 6, Sl St to beginning stitch, Ch 1 [12]

3. (SC, Inc) x 6, Sl St to beginning stitch, Ch 1 [18]

4. (SC, Inc, SC) x 6, Sl St to beginning stitch, Ch 1 [24]

5. (SC 3, Inc) x 6, Sl St to beginning stitch, Ch 1 [30]

6. (SC 2, Inc, SC 2) x 6, Sl St to beginning stitch, Ch 1 [36]

7–10. (4 rows of) SC 36, Sl St to beginning stitch, Ch 1 [36]

11. BLO [(HDC, HDC Inc) x 18], Sl St to beginning stitch, Ch 1 [54]

12. (HDC, FP Triple Crochet) x 27, Sl St to beginning stitch [54]

Fasten off with short yarn tail.

Part 2: Mushroom Cap
Color Yarn

1. Attach the yarn to the Back Loop of the first stitch of the final row of Part 1, BLO [(SC 5, Inc) x 9], Sl St to beginning stitch, Ch 1 [63]

2. (SC 3, Inc, SC 3) x 9, Sl St to beginning stitch, Ch 1 [72]

3-5. (3 rows of) SC 72, Sl St to beginning stitch, Ch 1 [72]

6. (SC 5, Dec, SC 5) x 6, Sl St to beginning stitch, Ch 1 [66]

7. SC 66, Sl St to beginning stitch, Ch 1 [66]

8. (SC 9, Dec) x 6, Sl St to beginning stitch, Ch 1 [60]

9. SC 60, Sl St to beginning stitch, Ch 1 [60]

10. (SC 4, Dec, SC 4) x 6, Sl St to beginning stitch, Ch 1 [54]

11. (SC 7, Dec) x 6, Sl St to beginning stitch, Ch 1 [48]

Standing Body Style 1, Arm Style 1, Round Mushroom Cap

12. (SC 3, Dec, SC 3) x 6, Sl St to beginning stitch, Ch 1 [42]
13. (SC 5, Dec) x 6, Sl St to beginning stitch, Ch 1 [36]
14. (SC 2, Dec, SC 2) x 6, Sl St to beginning stitch, Ch 1 [30]
15. (SC 3, Dec) x 6, Sl St to beginning stitch, Ch 1 [24]

At this point, stuff the Mushroom Cap very lightly. Fill in the space around the edge of the cap in the shape of a donut. The hat will use a small amount of stuffing in the center, above the concave space that will fit on the head of the Impkin. Do not overstuff. Fill out the shape of the cap, but do not warp the shaping. Err on the side of less stuffing.

16. (SC, Dec, SC) x 6, Sl St to beginning stitch, Ch 1 [18]
17. (SC, Dec) x 6, Sl St to beginning stitch, Ch 1 [12]

18. Dec x 6, Sl St to beginning stitch [6]

Fasten off with 12 in/30.5 cm yarn tail.

Assembly

1. Sew the hole shut with the yarn tail and weave in the end.
2. Place the hat on the head of the Impkin. Sew to attach using either the Impkin Body Color Yarn or the color of the underside of the Mushroom Cap. If the Mushroom Cap is too puffy, remove some stuffing. Weave in ends.

3. If you want to add dots over the Mushroom Cap, take an accent color and sew small single stitches evenly all across the cap, as explained in the Strawberry Stem Cap Assembly on page 109.

CURVED POINTED HAT

Edging Color Yarn: Approximately 6 yd/5.5 m total

Main Cap Color Yarn: Approximately 19 yd/17.25 m total

Part 1: Edging Color Yarn

1. Starting with a long enough yarn tail to weave in later, Ch 4, Turn, starting in the second Ch from hook, SC 3, Ch 1, Turn [3]
2–33. (32 rows of) BLO [SC 3], Ch 1, Turn [3]

34. Without twisting your work, hold Row 1 against your current work and Sl St 3 through both sides at the same time [3]

Fasten off with 12 in/30.5 cm yarn tail.

Part 2: Main Cap Color Yarn

1. Attach the yarn to any stitch on the side of the band you created from Part 1 (I prefer to attach the yarn closer to the seam created in Row 34), SC 34 around, one in each row from Part 1, Sl St to beginning stitch, Ch 1 [34]

2. SC 34, Sl St to beginning stitch, Ch 1 [34]

3. (SC 15, Dec) x 2, Sl St to beginning stitch, Ch 1 [32]

4. (SC 7, Dec, SC 7) x 2, Sl St to beginning stitch, Ch 1 [30]

5. (SC 13, Dec) x 2, Sl St to beginning stitch, Ch 1 [28]

6. (SC 6, Dec, SC 6) x 2, Sl St to beginning stitch, Ch 1 [26]

7. (SC 11, Dec) x 2, Sl St to beginning stitch, Ch 1 [24]

8. (SC 5, Dec, SC 5) x 2, Sl St to beginning stitch, Ch 1 [22]

9. (SC 9, Dec) x 2, Sl St to beginning stitch, Ch 1 [20]

10. (SC 4, Dec, SC 4) x 2, Sl St to beginning stitch, Ch 1 [18]

11. (SC 7, Dec) x 2, Sl St to beginning stitch, Ch 1 [16]

12. (SC 3, Dec, SC 3) x 2, Sl St to beginning stitch, Ch 1 [14]

13. (SC 5, Dec) x 2, Sl St to beginning stitch, Ch 1 [12]

14. (SC 2, Dec, SC 2) x 2, Sl St to beginning stitch, Ch 1 [10]

15. SC 3, Dec, SC, Inc, SC, Dec, Sl St to beginning stitch, Ch 1 [9]

16. Dec, SC 3, Inc, SC 3, Sl St to beginning stitch, Ch 1 [9]

17. Dec, SC 2, Inc, SC 2, Dec, Sl St to beginning stitch, Ch 1 [8]

18. Dec, SC 2, <Dec>, SC 2, Dec, Sl St to beginning stitch, Ch 1 [7]

19. Dec, SC, Inc, SC, Dec, Sl St to beginning stitch, Ch 1 [6]

20. Dec, SC, <Dec>, SC, Dec, Sl St to beginning stitch, Ch 1 [5]

21. Dec, Inc, Dec, Sl St to beginning stitch [4]

Fasten off with 12 in/30.5 cm yarn tail. You can use this tail to sew the hole shut. You can optionally attach a pom-pom to the end of the hat tip!

Assembly

Place the hat on the head of the Impkin. You do not have to sew to attach if you want the hat to be removable. Sew to attach using yarn tails if you want it to be a permanent attachment and weave in ends.

LEAF TOPPER

Leaf Color Yarn:
Approximately 18.5 yd/17 m total

1. Starting with a long enough yarn tail to weave in later, Ch 19, Turn, starting in the second Ch from hook, SC 6, HDC 6, DC 3, HDC 2, SC, Ch 20, Turn [18]

2. Starting in the second Ch from hook, SC 5, HDC 5, DC 3, HDC 2, SC, Ch 18, Turn [16]

> In this and following rows, you will not always use all the available chain stitches.

3. Starting in the second Ch from hook, SC 4, HDC 4, DC 3, HDC 2, SC, Ch 16, Turn [14]

4. Starting in the second Ch from hook, SC 4, HDC 4, DC 2, HDC, SC, Ch 14, Turn [12]

5. Starting in the second Ch from hook, SC 3, HDC 3, DC 2, HDC, SC, Ch 1, Turn [10]

> These first 5 rows create the base, or inner parts, of the 5 leaves. The next rows create the outer edges of the leaves and are worked around the entire edge of the leaves and into the unworked chains between the leaves.

Standing Body
Style 1,
Arm Style 1,
Leaf Topper

6. Working back along the leaf you made in Row 5, HDC 3, DC 3, HDC 3, Triple SC Inc in the last available stitch, continue working into the base chain of the leaf, HDC 3, DC 3, HDC 3, Sl St in the center of the 3 chain stitches between the Row 5 leaf and the Row 4 leaf [22]

7. Working back along the leaf you made in Row 4, HDC 3, DC 4, HDC 4, Triple SC Inc in the last available stitch, continue working into the base chain of the leaf, HDC 4, DC 4, HDC 3, Sl St in the center of the 3 chain stitches between the Row 4 leaf and the Row 3 leaf [26]

8. Working back along the leaf you made in Row 3, HDC 4, DC 4, HDC 4, SC, Triple SC Inc in the last available stitch, continue working into the base chain of the leaf, SC, HDC 4, DC 4, HDC 4, Sl St in the center of the 3 chain stitches between the Row 3 leaf and the Row 2 leaf [30]

9. Working back along the leaf you made in Row 2, HDC 4, DC 6, HDC 4, SC, Triple SC Inc in the last available stitch, continue working into the base chain of the leaf, SC, HDC 4, DC 6, HDC 4, Sl St in the center of the 3 chain stitches between the Row 2 leaf and the Row 1 leaf [34]

10. Working back along the leaf you made in Row 1, HDC 4, DC 7, HDC 5, SC, Triple SC Inc in the last available stitch, continue working into the base chain of the leaf, SC, HDC 5, DC 7, HDC 4 [37]

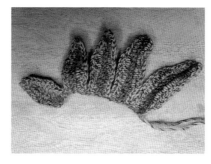

Fasten off with 24 in/61 cm yarn tail.

Assembly

Starting with the longest leaf, roll the base of the leaves up on themselves. Pin the rolled-up part centered on the top of the head of the Impkin. Sew to attach and weave in ends.

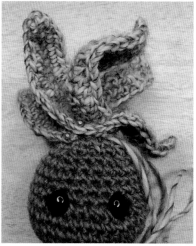

LONG, CURLY MANE

Mane Color Yarn:
Approximately 24 yd/22 m total

> For tight curls (as shown in photos), keep your chain stitches fairly tight.

1. Starting with a yarn tail long enough to weave in later, Ch 25, Turn, starting in the second Ch from hook, Inc x 24, Turn [48]

2. Ch 25, Turn, starting in the second Ch from hook, Inc x 24, Ch 1, Turn [48]

3. BLO [SC 2], Ch 25, Turn, starting in the second Ch from hook, Inc x 24, BLO [SC 2], Ch 1, Turn [52]

4. BLO [SC 3], Ch 25, Turn, starting in the second Ch from hook, Inc x 24, BLO [SC 3], Ch 1, Turn [54]

5. BLO [SC 3], Ch 25, Turn, starting in the second Ch from hook, Inc x 24, BLO [SC 3], Ch 1, Turn [54]

6. BLO [SC 3], Ch 25, Turn, starting in the second Ch from hook, Inc x 24, BLO [SC 3], Ch 1, Turn [54]

7. BLO [SC 3], Ch 25, Turn, starting in the second Ch from hook, Inc x 24, BLO [SC 3] [54]

Fasten off with 24 in/61 cm yarn tail.

Assembly

Pin the mane to attach it to the center line of the head, starting mid-forehead and extending back along the center of the head to the nape of the neck on the Impkin. You can add more than one layer of mane for a thicker/fuller look. You should also pin ears on at this time and figure out placement for all other ornaments (like horns, for example). Sew to attach and weave in ends.

BEING MADE BY HUMANS, HANGING AROUND HUMANS, INVESTIGATING AND EXPLORING THE HUMANS' WORLDS . . . IT'S NO WONDER THAT IMPKINS COME TO BE INTERESTED IN UNDERSTANDING AND MIMICKING HUMAN MANNERISMS, HUMAN ACCESSORIES, AND HUMAN STYLES. THEY MAY NOT ALWAYS KNOW EXACTLY WHAT THIS STRAPPY BAG OVER THEIR SHOULDERS IS FOR . . . BUT THEY KNOW THEY LIKE THE COLOR AND FEEL.

– Notes from the field, L. Mossgrove

SHORT-PIECED MANE/MOHAWK

Mane Color Yarn:
Approximately 8 yd/7.25 m total

Part 1

Starting with a long enough yarn tail to weave in later, Ch 25, starting in the second Ch from Hook, SC 24 [24]

Fasten off with 12 in/30.5 cm yarn tail.

Part 2

1. Cut 24 to 48 2-in/5-cm (or however long you want) pieces of yarn for the mane/mohawk.

2. Using 1 or 2 strands at a time, fold the yarn in half.

3. Insert the hook in the stitch you desire to attach the hair.

4. Loop the strand(s) over the hook at the strand's halfway point.

5. Pull that strand through the stitch the hook was inserted into, and pull up enough that you have a loop.

6. Loop the tail of the yarn strand over your hook.

7. Pull the end of the yarn strands all the way through the loop to create a knot, being careful to keep the ends of the strand even with each other. Pull the knot tight.

8. After attaching all the strands, you can optionally brush and/or trim the mane.

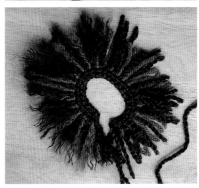

Standing Body Style 2, Arm Style 1, Short-Pieced Mane/Mohawk, Short and Pointy Horns, Messenger Bag

Standing Body
Style 2,
Arm Style 1,
Short-Pieced Mane/
Mohawk, Short and
Pointy Horns,
Messenger Bag

Assembly

Pin the mane to attach it to the center line of the head, starting mid-forehead and extending back along the center of the head to the nape of the neck on the Impkin. Sew to attach and weave in ends.

PIECED LION'S MANE

Mane Color Yarn: Approximately 15 yd/13.75 m total

This particular hairstyle is heavy. If you do not reinforce the neck of the Impkin with some kind of wire, dowel, or the like, then the head will be too heavy to be supported by the neck. If you're okay with a floppy/droopy-headed Impkin, that's fine. If you're not, it is important to reinforce the inside of the neck so that the head is held up.

Using the instructions in the Short-Pieced Mane/Mohawk pattern (Part 2 on pages 90–91), cut pieces of yarn about 5 in/12.5 cm in length (or the length of the arm span of the Impkin) and attach them all around the edge of the face, including in front of the neck, under the chin, and all over the back of the head. Trim and brush out if desired.

Optional Lion Embroidered Face

1. Use black embroidery thread or lace weight yarn (or unply/untwist some worsted weight yarn and use 1 or 2 strands of it) to embroider a broad, flat-topped triangle on the center of the face, between the eyes, with the top edge of the triangle aligned with the bottom edge of the safety eyes.

2. Then embroider a small, upside-down Y shape below the triangle nose. Weave in ends.

IMPKINS DON'T EVER HAVE TO LOOK ANY PARTICULAR WAY. FOR EVERY IMPKIN OUT THERE WITH A HAT, THERE'S ONE WITH A TAIL. FOR EVERY IMPKIN WITH EARS, THERE'S ONE WITH A CUTE LITTLE NOSE. IMPKINS LOVE MEETING EACH OTHER AND SEEING JUST HOW DIFFERENT THEY ALL CAN BE, JUST AS MUCH AS THEY LOVE FEELING SPECIAL IN THEIR CRAFTERS' EYES.

– Notes from the field, L. Mossgrove

Standing Body
Style 2,
Arm Style 1,
Pieced Lion's
Mane, Lion Tail

TOP HAT

**Hat Color Yarn:
Approximately 15 yd/13.75 m
total**

1. Starting with a long enough yarn tail to weave in later, SC 6 in Magic Circle, Sl St to beginning stitch, Ch 1 [6]

2. Inc x 6, Sl St to beginning stitch, Ch 1 [12]

3. (SC, Inc) x 6, Sl St to beginning stitch, Ch 1 [18]

4. (SC, Inc, SC) x 6, Sl St to beginning stitch, Ch 1 [24]

5. BLO [SC 24], Sl St to beginning stitch, Ch 1 [24]

6. (SC 3, Dec, SC 3) x 3, Sl St to beginning stitch, Ch 1 [21]

7. SC 21, Sl St to beginning stitch, Ch 1 [21]

8. SC 21, Sl St to beginning stitch, Ch 1 [21]

9. (SC 5, Dec) x 3, Sl St to beginning stitch, Ch 1 [18]

10. SC 18, Sl St to beginning stitch, Ch 1 [18]

11. SC 18, Sl St to beginning stitch, Ch 1 [18]

12. FLO [(SC, Inc, SC) x 6], Sl St to beginning stitch, Ch 1 [24]

13. (SC 3, Inc) x 6, Sl St to beginning stitch, Ch 1 [30]

14. (SC 2, Inc, SC 2) x 6, Sl St to beginning stitch [36]

Fasten off with 12 in/30.5 cm yarn tail.

Assembly

1. If you plan to permanently sew the hat to the head of your Impkin, light stuffing with fiberfill is optional before you pin to attach.

2. You can optionally decorate the hat with a ribbon—around the hat just above the brim—or a couple of tiny flowers, or both. Or you can make a hatband: Starting with a yarn tail long enough to weave in later, Ch 21, starting in the second Ch from hook, SC 20. Fasten off with 18 in/45.75 cm yarn tail and pin in place just above the brim of the hat. Sew the ornamentation to attach and weave in the end.

3. Pin in place on the head of the Impkin and sew to attach using the yarn tail. Weave in the ends.

Standing Body
Style 2,
Arm Style 2,
Top Hat, Bow Tie

SOME IMPKINS SHARE THEIR CRAFTERS' PROCLIVITY FOR NATURE, FOR THINGS GREEN AND GROWING AND BEAUTIFUL. THEY CAN SIT FOR HOURS AND HOURS, SOAKING IN THE SUN AND GENTLY SWAYING IN THE BREEZE. OUT OF POLITENESS TOWARD THEIR CRAFTERS, THEY TRY NOT TO GROW ROOTS OR SHOOT UP INTO THE SKY ON STALKS OF GREEN, BUT SOMETIMES THEY CAN'T HELP THEMSELVES.

– Notes from the field, L. Mossgrove

FLOWER HAT

Petal Color Yarn:
Approximately 10 yd/9.25 m total

Flower Center Color Yarn:
Approximately 20 yd/18.25 m total

Part 1: Petal Color Yarn

1. Starting with a long enough yarn tail to weave in later, (Ch 7, starting in the second Ch from hook, Sl St, HDC, DC, Half Trip, Half Trip, DC) x 10, Ch 2 [6 stitches per petal]

2. (Ch 9, starting in the second Ch from hook, Sl St, HDC, DC, Half Trip, Triple Crochet, Triple Crochet, Half Trip, DC) x 10 [8 stitches per petal]

Part 2: Flower Center Color Yarn

1. Starting with a long enough yarn tail to weave in later, SC 6 in Magic Circle, Sl St to beginning stitch, Ch 1 [6]

2. (Inc, Ch 4) x 6, Sl St to beginning stitch, Ch 1 [12, plus 6 Ch 4 loops]

3. (SC, Ch 4, Inc) x 6, Sl St to beginning stitch, Ch 1 [18, plus 6 Ch 4 loops]

> In this row and all following rows, you will skip and not crochet into the Ch 4 instruction from the previous row. Keep the Ch 4 loops oriented to the front/right side of the work. They will create texture that looks like a flower center/seeds. Do not crochet into the Ch 4 instructions.

4. (SC 2, Ch 4, Inc) x 6, Sl St to beginning stitch, Ch 1 [24, plus 6 Ch 4 loops]

5. (SC, Ch 4, SC 2, Ch 4, Inc) x 6, Sl St to beginning stitch, Ch 1 [30, plus 12 Ch 4 loops]

6. (SC 2, Inc, SC 2) x 6, Sl St to beginning stitch [36]

Fasten off with 24 in/61 cm yarn tail.

Fasten off with 18 in/45.75 cm yarn tail.

Sitting Body
Style 2,
Arm Style 2,
Flower Hat

Assembly

1. Pin Part 2 of the Flower Hat on the back of the Impkin's head, as shown. Do not yet sew to attach.

2. Pin Part 1 of the Flower Hat in place starting with the shorter petals, wrapping it around the outer edge of Part 2. Once you reach the end of the short petals, continue to wrap Part 1 so that the longer petals are layered under the shorter petals. Pin it in place securely, verify placement.

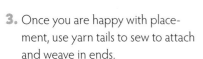

3. Once you are happy with placement, use yarn tails to sew to attach and weave in ends.

WIDE CROWN

Hat Color Yarn: Approximately 6 yd/5.5 m total

1. Starting with a long enough yarn tail to weave in later, Ch 28, Sl St to the beginning Ch stitch to create a circle of chain stitches, Ch 1

> Be careful not to twist the chain stitches when you create the circle.

2. SC 28, Sl St to beginning stitch, Ch 1 [28]

> In Row 2, you will SC in each of the chain stitches from Row 1 all the way around the circle.

3. SC 28, DO NOT "Sl St to beginning stitch, Ch 1," continue in spiral [28]

4. (Sl St 2, Ch 2, Sl St in the second Ch from hook, Sl St 2, Ch 3, Sl St in the second Ch from hook, SC in the next Ch) x 7, Sl St in the same stitch you first slip stitched into in this row [49]

Fasten off with 12 in/30.5 cm yarn tail.

SMALL CROWN

Hat Color Yarn: Approximately 4 yd/3.75 m total

1. Starting with a long enough yarn tail to weave in later, Ch 16, Sl St to the beginning Ch stitch to create a circle of chain stitches, Ch 1

> Be careful not to twist the chain stitches when you create the circle.

2. SC 16, Sl St to beginning stitch, Ch 1 [16]

> In Row 2 you will SC in each of the chain stitches from Row 1 all the way around the circle.

3. SC 16, DO NOT "Sl St to beginning stitch, Ch 1," continue in spiral [16]

4. (Sl St 2, Ch 2, Sl St in the second Ch from hook, Sl St 2, Ch 3, Sl St in the second Ch from hook, SC in the next Ch) x 4, Sl St in the same stitch you first slip stitched into in this row [28]

Fasten off with 12 in/30.5 cm yarn tail.

Assembly

Pin in place on the head of the Impkin. Once you are satisfied with placement, sew to attach using yarn tails and weave in ends.

Assembly

Pin in place on the head of the Impkin. Once you are satisfied with placement, sew to attach using yarn tails and weave in ends.

Sitting Body
Style 1,
Arm Style 1,
Ribbed Belly,
Wide Crown

Sitting Body
Style 2,
Arm Style 2,
Small Crown, Tutu

SMOOTH WIZARD/WITCH HAT

Hat Color Yarn:
Approximately 37 yd/33.75 m total

1. Starting with a long enough yarn tail to weave in later, SC 5 in Magic Circle, Sl St to beginning stitch, Ch 1 [5]

2. SC 4, Inc, Sl St to beginning stitch, Ch 1 [6]

3. (SC, Inc, SC) x 2, Sl St to beginning stitch, Ch 1 [8]

4. (SC 3, Inc) x 2, Sl St to beginning stitch, Ch 1 [10]

5. (SC 2, Inc, SC 2) x 2, Sl St to beginning stitch, Ch 1 [12]

6. (SC 5, Inc) x 2, Sl St to beginning stitch, Ch 1 [14]

7. (SC 3, Inc, SC 3) x 2, Sl St to beginning stitch, Ch 1 [16]

8. (SC 7, Inc) x 2, Sl St to beginning stitch, Ch 1 [18]

9. (SC 4, Inc, SC 4) x 2, Sl St to beginning stitch, Ch 1 [20]

10. (SC 9, Inc) x 2, Sl St to beginning stitch, Ch 1 [22]

11. (SC 5, Inc, SC 5) x 2, Sl St to beginning stitch, Ch 1 [24]

12. (SC 11, Inc) x 2, Sl St to beginning stitch, Ch 1 [26]

13. (SC 6, Inc, SC 6) x 2, Sl St to beginning stitch, Ch 1 [28]

14. (SC 13, Inc) x 2, Sl St to beginning stitch, Ch 1 [30]

15. (SC 7, Inc, SC 7) x 2, Sl St to beginning stitch, Ch 1 [32]

16. (SC 15, Inc) x 2, Sl St to beginning stitch, Ch 1 [34]

17. (SC 8, Inc, SC 8) x 2, Sl St to beginning stitch, Ch 1 [36]

18. FLO [(SC 5, Inc) x 6], Sl St to beginning stitch, Ch 1 [42]

19. (SC 3, Inc, SC 3) x 6, Sl St to beginning stitch, Ch 1 [48]

20. (SC 7, Inc) x 6, Sl St to beginning stitch, Ch 1 [54]

21. (SC 4, Inc, SC 4) x 6, Sl St to beginning stitch, Ch 1 [60]

22. (SC 9, Inc) x 6, Sl St to beginning stitch, Ch 1 [66]

23. (SC 5, Inc, SC 5) x 6, Sl St to beginning stitch [72]

Fasten off with 12 in/30.5 cm yarn tail.

Assembly

It is optional to sew this hat to attach to the head of the Impkin. If you want the Impkin to wear it as removable clothing, weave in the yarn tail of the hat. If you want the Impkin to permanently wear this hat, then pin to attach to the head and, once you are satisfied with placement, sew it to attach using the yarn tail and weave in the end.

WRINKLED WIZARD/WITCH HAT

Hat Color Yarn:
Approximately 67 yd/61.25 m total

1. Starting with a long enough yarn tail to weave in later, SC 5 in Magic Circle, Sl St to beginning stitch, Ch 1 [5]

2. SC 5, Sl St to beginning stitch, Ch 1 [5]

3. SC 4, Inc, Sl St to beginning stitch, Ch 1 [6]

4. SC 6, Sl St to beginning stitch, Ch 1 [6]

5. (SC, Inc, SC) x 2, Sl St to beginning stitch, Ch 1 [8]

6. SC 8, Sl St to beginning stitch, Ch 1 [8]

7. (SC 3, Inc) x 2, Sl St to beginning stitch, Ch 1 [10]

8. SC 10, Sl St to beginning stitch, Ch 1 [10]

9. (SC 2, Inc, SC 2) x 2, Sl St to beginning stitch, Ch 1 [12]

Standing Body
Style 1,
Arm Style 1,
Smooth Wizard/
Witch Hat

10. SC 12, Sl St to beginning stitch, Ch 1 [12]

11. (SC 5, Inc) x 2, Sl St to beginning stitch, Ch 1 [14]

12. SC 14, Sl St to beginning stitch, Ch 1 [14]

13. (SC 3, Inc, SC 3) x 2, Sl St to beginning stitch, Ch 1 [16]

14. SC 16, Sl St to beginning stitch, Ch 1 [16]

15. (SC 7, Inc) x 2, Sl St to beginning stitch, Ch 1 [18]

16. SC 18, Sl St to beginning stitch, Ch 1 [18]

17. (SC 4, Inc, SC 4) x 2, Sl St to beginning stitch, Ch 1 [20]

18. SC 20, Sl St to beginning stitch, Ch 1 [20]

19. (SC 9, Inc) x 2, Sl St to beginning stitch, Ch 1 [22]

20. SC 22, Sl St to beginning stitch, Ch 1 [22]

21. (SC 5, Inc, SC 5) x 2, Sl St to beginning stitch, Ch 1 [24]

22. SC 24, Sl St to beginning stitch, Ch 1 [24]

23. (SC 11, Inc) x 2, Sl St to beginning stitch, Ch 1 [26]

24. SC 26, Sl St to beginning stitch, Ch 1 [26]

25. (SC 6, Inc, SC 6) x 2, Sl St to beginning stitch, Ch 1 [28]

26. SC 28, Sl St to beginning stitch, Ch 1 [28]

27. (SC 13, Inc) x 2, Sl St to beginning stitch, Ch 1 [30]

28. SC 30, Sl St to beginning stitch, Ch 1 [30]

29. (SC 7, Inc, SC 7) x 2, Sl St to beginning stitch, Ch 1 [32]

30. SC 32, Sl St to beginning stitch, Ch 1 [32]

31. (SC 15, Inc) x 2, Sl St to beginning stitch, Ch 1 [34]

32. SC 34, Sl St to beginning stitch, Ch 1 [34]

33. (SC 8, Inc, SC 8) x 2, Sl St to beginning stitch, Ch 1 [36]

34. SC 36, Sl St to beginning stitch, Ch 1 [36]

35. FLO [(SC 5, Inc) x 6], Sl St to beginning stitch, Ch 1 [42]

36. (SC 3, Inc, SC 3) x 6, Sl St to beginning stitch, Ch 1 [48]

37. (SC 7, Inc) x 6, Sl St to beginning stitch, Ch 1 [54]

38. (SC 4, Inc, SC 4) x 6, Sl St to beginning stitch, Ch 1 [60]

39. (SC 9, Inc) x 6, Sl St to beginning stitch, Ch 1 [66]

40. (SC 5, Inc, SC 5) x 6, Sl St to beginning stitch [72]

Fasten off with 24 in/61 cm yarn tail.

Assembly

1. The brim of the hat should remain as is, but the top part of the hat can be squished/wrinkled down to create a folded, wonky look. Use the yarn tail to secure the folds in place as you want.

2. It is optional to sew this hat to attach to the head of the Impkin. If you want the Impkin to wear it as removable clothing, weave in the yarn tail of the hat. If you want the Impkin to permanently wear this hat, then pin to attach to the head and, once you are satisfied with placement, sew it to attach using the yarn tail and weave in the end.

AS YOU CRAFT YOUR IMPKIN, PAY ATTENTION TO HOW
YOUR CHOICES WILL AFFECT THEIR DIETARY NEEDS. TO
MAINTAIN THEIR ORIGINAL COLORATION, MANY IMPKINS SEEK
EQUIVALENTLY COLORED FOODS, SO BE SURE TO KEEP SOME
AROUND THAT YOUR IMPKIN MIGHT NOSH IN TIMES OF GREAT
HUNGER. OTHERWISE, THEY HAVE BEEN KNOWN TO CONSUME
APPROPRIATELY COLORED SOCKS. ONCE AN IMPKIN DEVELOPS
A REAL TASTE FOR SOCKS, YOU WILL FIND IT MIGHTILY DIFFICULT
TO MAINTAIN FULL PAIRS—MANY A CRAFTER IS FORCED NOW TO
WEAR ODDLY MISMATCHED SOCKS BECAUSE THEY FORGOT TO
LEAVE OUT FOOD THAT MATCHED THEIR IMPKIN'S HUES!

– Notes from the field, L. Mossgrove

Sitting Body
Style 2,
Arm Style 2,
Strawberry
Stem Cap

STRAWBERRY STEM CAP

Cap Color Yarn:
Approximately 7 yd/6.5 m total

1. Starting with a yarn tail that you can tuck inside the strawberry stem, SC 5 in Magic Circle, Sl St to beginning stitch, Ch 1 [5]

2. BLO [SC 5], Sl St to beginning stitch, Ch 1 [5]

3–7. (5 rows of) SC 5, Sl St to beginning stitch, Ch 1 [5]

8. FLO [Inc x 5], Sl St to beginning stitch, Ch 1 [10]

9. (SC, Inc) x 5, Do not "Sl St to beginning Stitch, Ch 1," continue in spiral [15]

10. (Sl St, Ch 7, starting in the second Ch from hook, Sl St, HDC, DC, Half Trip, Half Trip, DC, Skip 1 stitch from Row 9, Sl St in the next stitch) x 5 [40]

Fasten off with 18 in/45.75 cm yarn tail.

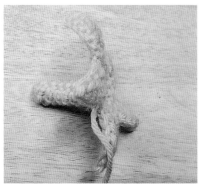

Assembly

1. Pin in place on the head of the Impkin. Once you are satisfied with placement, sew to attach using yarn tails and weave in ends.

2. Use a light yellow, white, or cream yarn to embroider little stitches all over the center of the body of the Impkin, as shown. Place these stitches evenly across the body to imitate strawberry seeds.

Standing Body
Style 1,
Arm Style 1,
Strawberry
Stem Cap

MANDRAKE TOPPER

Root Color Yarn: Approximately 9 yd/8.25 m total

Leaf Color Yarn: Approximately 5 yd/4.5 m total

Alternatively, instead of making the Mandrake Topper for a Mandrake, you can make the Leaf Topper and follow the assembly instructions to add roots to the hands and feet of your Impkin.

Part 1: Root Color Yarn

1. SC 5 in Magic Circle, Sl St to beginning stitch, Ch 1 [5]

2. SC 5, Sl St to beginning stitch, Ch 1 [5]

3. SC 5, Sl St to beginning stitch, Ch 1 [5]

4. SC 2, Inc, SC 2, Sl St to beginning stitch, Ch 1 [6]

5. SC 6, Sl St to beginning stitch, Ch 1 [6]

6. SC 6, Sl St to beginning stitch [6]

Fasten off with short yarn tail.

Part 2: Root Color Yarn

1. SC 5 in Magic Circle, Sl St to beginning stitch, Ch 1 [5]

2. SC 5, Sl St to beginning stitch, Ch 1 [5]

3. SC 5, Sl St to beginning stitch, Ch 1 [5]

4. SC 5, Sl St to beginning stitch, Ch 1 [5]

5. SC 2, Inc, SC 2, Sl St to beginning stitch, Ch 1 [6]

6. SC 6, Sl St to beginning stitch, Ch 1 [6]

7. SC 6, Sl St to beginning stitch, Ch 1 [6]

8. SC 6, Sl St to beginning stitch, Ch 1 [6]

9. SC 6, starting into the first stitch on Part 1, SC 6, SC in the same stitch you last single crocheted into on Part 2, Sl St to beginning stitch, Ch 1 [13]

10. SC 2, Inc, SC 5, Inc, SC 2, Dec, Sl St to beginning stitch, Ch 1 [14]

11. (SC 6, Inc) x 2, Sl St to beginning stitch, Ch 1 [16]

12. (SC 3, Inc) x 4, Sl St to beginning stitch [20]

Fasten off with 12 in/30.5 cm yarn tail.

Part 3: Leaf Color Yarn

1. Starting with a long enough yarn tail to weave in later, Ch 4, starting in the second Ch from hook, SC 3, Ch 1, Turn [3]

2. SC, HDC, SC, Ch 3, starting in the second Ch from hook, Sl St, HDC, continuing to crochet down the opposite side of the starting chain in Row 1, SC, HDC, SC, fold the leaf lengthwise and Sl St to the beginning stitch of this row [7]

3. Ch 6, starting in the second Ch from hook, SC 5, Ch 1, Turn [5]

4. SC, HDC, DC, HDC, SC, Ch 3, starting in the second Ch from hook, Sl St, HDC, continuing to crochet down the opposite side of the starting chain in Row 3, SC, HDC, DC, HDC, SC, fold the leaf lengthwise and Sl St to the beginning stitch of this row [11]

5. Ch 8, starting in the second Ch from hook, SC 7, Ch 1, Turn [7]

6. SC, HDC, DC, Half Trip, DC, HDC, SC, Ch 3, starting in the second Ch from hook, Sl St, HDC, continuing to crochet down the opposite side of the starting chain in Row 5, SC, HDC, DC, Half Trip, DC, HDC, SC, fold the leaf lengthwise and Sl St to the beginning stitch of this row [15]

Fasten off with 12 in/30.5 cm yarn tail.

You can repeat Part 3 as many times as you want to create sets of leaves to decorate Parts 1 and 2 as if they are part of a living, growing plant. You can also ONLY work Rows 1 and 2, or Rows 3 and 4, or Rows 5 and 6, or any combination of those sets of 2 rows to create different-size leaves.

Standing Body
Style 1,
Arm Style 2,
Mandrake Topper

Assembly

1. Stuff the piece created in Parts 1 and 2 medium-firm with fiberfill. Pin this to the top of the head of the Impkin and sew to attach using the yarn tail to seamlessly attach it to the head.

2. Pin the Part 3 leaves to the Parts 1 and 2 piece, sew to attach using yarn tails, and weave in ends.

3. Cut 2 pieces of 4-in/10.25-cm long yarn per limb and attach them to the hands and feet of the Impkin. Unwind the ply of the yarn. These pieces are meant to imitate roots.

4. Weave in any remaining ends.

VIKING HAT

Hat Color Yarn (gray recommended): Approximately 20 yd/18.25 m total

Horn Color Yarn (white recommended): Approximately 12 yd/11 m total

Hat Color 2 Yarn (gray recommended): Approximately 4 yd/3.75 m total

Part 1: Hat Color Yarn (Make 1)

1. Starting with a long enough yarn tail to weave in later, SC 6 in Magic Circle, Sl St to beginning stitch, Ch 1 [6]

2. Inc x 6, Sl St to beginning stitch, Ch 1 [12]

3. (SC, Inc) x 6, Sl St to beginning stitch, Ch 1 [18]

4. (SC, Inc, SC) x 6, Sl St to beginning stitch, Ch 1 [24]

5. (SC 3, Inc) x 6, Sl St to beginning stitch, Ch 1 [30]

6. (SC 2, Inc, SC 2) x 6, Sl St to beginning stitch, Ch 1 [36]

7–10. (4 rows of) SC 36, Sl St to beginning stitch, Ch 1 [36]

11. BLO [(SC, Small Bobble, SC) x 12], Sl St to beginning stitch, Ch 1 [36]

> To create the Small Bobble stitch in Row 11, YO, insert the hook in the next available stitch, YO, pull up, YO, insert the hook in the same stitch, YO, pull up, YO, pull through all remaining loops.

12. BLO [SC 36], Sl St to beginning stitch [36]

Fasten off with 18 in/45.75 cm yarn tail.

Part 2: Horn Color Yarn (Make 2)

1. SC 4 in Magic Circle, Sl St to beginning stitch, Ch 1 [4]

2. SC 3, Inc, Sl St to beginning stitch, Ch 1 [5]

3. SC 4, Inc, Sl St to beginning stitch, Ch 1 [6]

4. SC 5, Inc, Sl St to beginning stitch, Ch 1 [7]

5. SC 2, Dec, SC 2, Inc, Sl St to beginning stitch, Ch 1 [7]

6. SC 6, Inc, Sl St to beginning stitch, Ch 1 [8]

7. SC 7, Inc, Sl St to beginning stitch, Ch 1 [9]

8. SC 3, Dec, SC 3, Inc, Sl St to beginning stitch, Ch 1 [9]

9. SC 8, Inc, Sl St to beginning stitch, Ch 1 [10]

10. SC 9, Inc, Sl St to beginning stitch, Ch 1 [11]

11. SC 3, Dec, SC 4, Inc, SC, Sl St to beginning stitch [11]

Fasten off with 12 in/30.5 cm yarn tail.

Part 3: Hat Color Yarn (Make 2)

1. Starting with a long enough yarn tail to weave in later, Ch 13, Sl St to the beginning Ch stitch, without twisting the chain, to make a loop, Ch 1 [13]

2. SC 13, Sl St to beginning stitch

Fasten off with 12 in/30.5 cm yarn tail.

Assembly

1. It is optional to lightly stuff the Part 2 Horns with fiberfill. Pin the Part 2 Horns in place on either side of the Viking Hat you made in Part 1. Using the yarn tail, sew to attach to the hat. Weave in ends.

2. Slide the Part 3 loops down over each Horn and pin to the base of the horn. Using the yarn tail, sew to attach and weave in the ends.

3. It is optional to sew this hat to attach to the head of the Impkin. If you want the Impkin to wear it as removable clothing, weave in the yarn tail of the hat. If you want the Impkin to permanently wear this hat, then pin to attach to the head and, once you are satisfied with placement, sew it to attach using the yarn tail and weave in the end.

Standing Body
Style 2,
Arm Style 2,
Pumpkin
Stem Cap

PUMPKIN STEM CAP

Stem Color Yarn: Approximately 5 yd/4.5 m total

Tendril/Vine Color Yarn: Approximately 4 yd/3.75 m total

Part 1: Stem (Make 1)

1. HDC 6 in a Magic Circle, Sl St to beginning stitch, Ch 1 [6]
2. BLO [SC 6], Sl St to beginning stitch, Ch 1 [6]
3. SC 2, Dec, SC 2, Sl St to beginning stitch, Ch 1 [5]
4. SC 5, Sl St to beginning stitch, Ch 1 [5]
5. SC 5, Sl St to beginning stitch, Ch 1 [5]
6. SC 5, Sl St to beginning stitch, Ch 1 [5]
7. SC, Inc, SC, Inc, Inc, Sl St to beginning stitch, Ch 1 [8]
8. (HDC Inc, Ch 2, Sl St in the second Ch from hook) x 8, Sl St to beginning stitch [16]

Fasten off with 12 in/30.5 cm yarn tail.

Part 2: Tendrils/Vines (Make 1 or 2)

1. Starting with a long enough yarn tail to weave in later, Ch 21, starting in the second Ch from hook, Sl St, Inc x 19, Ch 15, Turn [38]
2. Starting in the second Ch from hook, Sl St, Inc x 13 [26]

Fasten off with 12 in/30.5 cm yarn tail.

Assembly

1. Pin the Stem in place on the top-center of the head of the Impkin, sew to attach using the yarn tail, and weave in the end.

2. Pin the Tendrils/Vines in place against the Stem, sew to attach using the yarn tail, and weave in the ends.

HOOD AND CAPE

Any Color Yarn:
Approximately 92 yd/84 m total

Part 1

1. Starting with a long enough yarn tail to weave in later, SC 6 in Magic Circle, Sl St to beginning stitch, Ch 1 [6]

2. Inc x 6, Sl St to beginning stitch, Ch 1 [12]

3. (SC, Inc) x 6, Sl St to beginning stitch, Ch 1 [18]

4. (SC, Inc, SC) x 6, Sl St to beginning stitch, Ch 1 [24]

5. (SC 3, Inc) x 6, Sl St to beginning stitch, Ch 1 [30]

6. (SC 2, Inc, SC 2) x 6, Sl St to beginning stitch, Ch 1 [36]

7. (SC 5, Inc) x 6, Sl St to beginning stitch, Ch 1 [42]

> Rows 8 to 17 are worked in rows, not rounds. You will not "Sl St to beginning stitch, Ch 1" in these rows; you will Ch 1, Turn at the end of each row.

8-17. (10 rows of) SC 42, Ch 1, Turn

18. SC 42

> Do not turn at the end of Row 18; follow the instructions at the beginning of Row 19 for where to crochet.

19. Working back along the unfinished edge that was created in the build-up of Rows 8 to 18, SC 24, Ch 1, Turn [24]

20. BLO [(SC, Inc) x 12], Ch 1, Turn [36]

21. SC 36, Ch 1, Turn [36]

22. (SC 5, Inc) x 6, Ch 1, Turn [42]

23. SC 42, Ch 1, Turn [42]

24. SC 42, Ch 1, Turn [42]

25. (SC 3, Inc, SC 3) x 6, Ch 1, Turn [48]

26-28. (3 rows of) SC 48, Ch 1, Turn [48]

29. (SC 7, Inc) x 6, Ch 1, Turn [54]

30-33. (4 rows of) SC 54, Ch 1, Turn [54]

34. (SC 4, Inc, SC 4) x 6, Ch 1, Turn [60]

35-39. (5 rows of) SC 60, Ch 1, Turn [60]

40. (SC 9, Inc) x 6, Ch 1 [66]

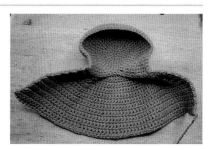

41. Working up the unfinished edge of the cape toward the hood, SC about 22 up to the BLO stitches at the start of the hood, SC 42 around the hood, SC about 22 back down the other edge of the cape, Ch 1 [about 86]

42. Optional: Working along the bottom edge of the cape, Skip 10 stitches, Sl St in the eleventh stitch, Sl St 44, working into the next available stitch AND the last available stitch on the cape edge at the same time, Sl St

Fasten off with 12 in/30.5 cm yarn tail.

Assembly

Pin in place on your Impkin. Use a matching piece of yarn to sew to attach at the neck. Weave in the ends. It is optional to weave a piece of yarn at the neck opening of the cape to make a tie for a removable item of clothing.

AN IMPKIN ALWAYS APPRECIATES VARIETY AND FASHION—ESPECIALLY WHEN THEY ARE THE ONE MADE FASHIONABLE. GIFT YOUR IMPKIN SOME KIND OF BOLD FASHION STATEMENT WHILE CRAFTING THEM, AND YOU WILL GIFT THEM A BOLD ESSENCE! EVEN IF THEY'RE A BIT SHY AROUND YOUR HOME, YOU CAN BE SURE THEY'RE SHOWING OFF ALL OVER THE IMPKINGDOM.

– Notes from the field, L. Mossgrove

Standing Body
Style 2,
Arm Style 1,
Hood and Cape

EVEN WITH THEIR EXCELLENT CONSTRUCTION AND FASHIONABLE COSTUMING, IMPKINS HAVE A PARTICULARLY IMPRESSIVE FACILITY FOR HIDING AND CAMOUFLAGE. GIVING THEM USEFUL ACCOUTREMENTS FOR HIDING IN PLAIN SIGHT ALLOWS THEM TO VENTURE EASILY OUT INTO THE WORLD—OR EVEN KEEP WATCH OVER THEIR FAVORITE BIG FOLK!

– Notes from the field, L. Mossgrove

POINTED MUSHROOM CAP

Underside Mushroom Cap Color Yarn: Approximately 36 yd/33 m total

Mushroom Cap Color Yarn: Approximately 54 yd/49.5 m total

This particular hat style is heavy. If you do not reinforce the neck of the Impkin with some kind of wire, dowel, or the like, then the head will be too heavy to be supported by the neck. If you are okay with a floppy/droopy-headed Impkin, then you do not need to use wire.

Part 1: Underside Mushroom Cap Color Yarn

1. SC 6 in Magic Circle, Sl St to beginning stitch, Ch 1 [6]
2. Inc x 6, Sl St to beginning stitch, Ch 1 [12]
3. (SC, Inc) x 6, Sl St to beginning stitch, Ch 1 [18]
4. (SC, Inc, SC) x 6, Sl St to beginning stitch, Ch 1 [24]
5. (SC 3, Inc) x 6, Sl St to beginning stitch, Ch 1 [30]
6. (SC 2, Inc, SC 2) x 6, Sl St to beginning stitch, Ch 1 [36]
7–10. (4 rows of) SC 36, Sl St to beginning stitch, Ch 1 [36]
11. BLO [(HDC, HDC Inc) x 18], Sl St to beginning stitch, Ch 1 [54]
12. (HDC Inc, FP Triple Crochet) x 27, Sl St to beginning stitch, Ch 1 [81]

13. (HDC 2, FP Triple Crochet) x 27, Sl St to beginning stitch [81]

Fasten off with short yarn tail.

Part 2: Mushroom Cap Color Yarn

1. SC 6 in Magic Circle, Sl St to beginning stitch, Ch 1 [6]
2. SC 6, Sl St to beginning stitch, Ch 1 [6]
3. Inc x 6, Sl St to beginning stitch, Ch 1 [12]
4. SC 12, Sl St to beginning stitch, Ch 1 [12]
5. (SC, Inc) x 6, Sl St to beginning stitch, Ch 1 [18]
6. SC 18, Sl St to beginning stitch, Ch 1 [18]
7. (SC, Inc) x 9, Sl St to beginning stitch, Ch 1 [27]
8. SC 27, Sl St to beginning stitch, Ch 1 [27]
9. (SC, Inc, SC) x 9, Sl St to beginning stitch, Ch 1 [36]

10. SC 36, Sl St to beginning stitch, Ch 1 [36]

11. (SC 3, Inc) x 9, Sl St to beginning stitch, Ch 1 [45]

12. SC 45, Sl St to beginning stitch, Ch 1 [45]

13. (SC 2, Inc, SC 2) x 9, Sl St to beginning stitch, Ch 1 [54]

14. SC 54, Sl St to beginning stitch, Ch 1 [54]

15. (SC 5, Inc) x 9, Sl St to beginning stitch, Ch 1 [63]

16. SC 63, Sl St to beginning stitch, Ch 1 [63]

17. (SC 3, Inc, SC 3) x 9, Sl St to beginning stitch, Ch 1 [72]

18. (SC 7, Inc) x 9, Sl St to beginning stitch, Ch 1 [81]

19. Hold Part 2 on top of Part 1 (wrong side to wrong side), working through both parts at the same time, SC 81 around, Sl St to beginning stitch [81]

There is no need to stuff this hat with fiberfill. It is optional to fill the top point of Part 2 of the Mushroom Cap with fiberfill. Do not overstuff the hat. Part 1 needs to be perfectly concave to sit on an Impkin's head.

Fasten off with yarn tail long enough to weave in.

Assembly

Pin in place on the head of the Impkin, sew to attach using the same color yarn as either the Impkin Body or Part 1 of the hat, and weave in the ends.

TWISTED MUSHROOM CAP

Underside Mushroom Cap Color Yarn: Approximately 36 yd/33 m total
Mushroom Cap Color Yarn: Approximately 58 yd/53 m total

This particular hat style is heavy. If you do not reinforce the neck of the Impkin with some kind of wire, dowel, or the like, then the head will be too heavy to be supported by the neck. If you are okay with a floppy/droopy-headed Impkin, then you do not need to use wire.

Part 1: Underside Mushroom Cap Color Yarn

1. SC 6 in Magic Circle, Sl St to beginning stitch, Ch 1 [6]
2. Inc x 6, Sl St to beginning stitch, Ch 1 [12]
3. (SC, Inc) x 6, Sl St to beginning stitch, Ch 1 [18]
4. (SC, Inc, SC) x 6, Sl St to beginning stitch, Ch 1 [24]
5. (SC 3, Inc) x 6, Sl St to beginning stitch, Ch 1 [30]
6. (SC 2, Inc, SC 2) x 6, Sl St to beginning stitch, Ch 1 [36]
7–10. (4 rows of) SC 36, Sl St to beginning stitch, Ch 1 [36]
11. BLO [(HDC, HDC Inc) x 18], Sl St to beginning stitch, Ch 1 [54]
12. (HDC Inc, FP Triple Crochet) x 27, Sl St to beginning stitch, Ch 1 [81]
13. (HDC 2, FP Triple Crochet) x 27, Sl St to beginning stitch [81]

Fasten off with short yarn tail.

Part 2: Mushroom Cap Color Yarn

1. SC 5 in Magic Circle, Sl St to beginning stitch, Ch 1 [5]
2. SC 5, Sl St to beginning stitch, Ch 1 [5]
3. Inc, SC 4, Sl St to beginning stitch, Ch 1 [6]
4. SC, Inc, SC 4, Sl St to beginning stitch, Ch 1 [7]
5. SC, Inc, SC, HDC 4, Sl St to beginning stitch, Ch 1 [8]
6. SC 2, Inc, SC 2, HDC 3, Sl St to beginning stitch, Ch 1 [9]
7. SC 2, Inc x 2, SC 2, HDC 3, Sl St to beginning stitch, Ch 1 [11]
8. SC 4, Inc, SC 4, Inc x 2, Sl St to beginning stitch, Ch 1 [14]
9. SC 2, HDC 6, SC 3, Inc x 2, SC, Sl St to beginning stitch, Ch 1 [16]
10. SC 3, HDC 4, SC 5, Inc x 2, SC 2, Sl St to beginning stitch, Ch 1 [18]
11. (SC 5, Inc) x 3, Sl St to beginning stitch, Ch 1 [21]
12. SC 12, (SC, Inc, SC) x 3, Sl St to beginning stitch, Ch 1 [24]
13. HDC 14, (SC, Inc, SC) x 3, HDC, Sl St to beginning stitch, Ch 1 [27]
14. (SC 4, Inc, SC 4) x 3, Sl St to beginning stitch, Ch 1 [30]
15. SC 2, (SC, Inc, SC) x 4, SC 2, HDC 14, Sl St to beginning stitch, Ch 1 [34]
16. SC 2, (SC, Inc, SC) x 5, SC 3, HDC 14, Sl St to beginning stitch, Ch 1 [39]
17. (SC 5, Inc) x 4, SC 5, HDC 2, HDC Inc, HDC 5, SC, Inc, Sl St to beginning stitch, Ch 1 [45]
18. SC 45, Sl St to beginning stitch, Ch 1 [45]
19. SC 25, HDC 20, Sl St to beginning stitch, Ch 1 [45]
20. HDC 25, (SC 3, Inc) x 5, Sl St to beginning stitch, Ch 1 [50]
21. SC, HDC 23, SC 26, Sl St to beginning stitch, Ch 1 [50]
22. (SC 9, Inc) x 5, Sl St to beginning stitch, Ch 1 [55]

23. (SC 5, Inc, SC 5) x 5, Sl St to beginning stitch, Ch 1 [60]

24. (SC 11, Inc) x 5, Sl St to beginning stitch, Ch 1 [65]

25. (SC 6, Inc, SC 6) x 5, Sl St to beginning stitch, Ch 1 [70]

26. (SC 13, Inc) x 5, Sl St to beginning stitch, Ch 1 [75]

27. (SC 7, Inc, SC 7) x 4, SC 7, Inc, SC 6, Inc, Sl St to beginning stitch, Ch 1 [81]

28. Hold Part 2 on top of Part 1 (wrong side to wrong side), working through both parts at the same time, (SC 4, Inc, SC 4) x 9 around, Sl St to beginning stitch [90]

There is no need to stuff this hat with fiberfill. It is optional to fill the top point of Part 2 of the Mushroom Cap with fiberfill. Do not overstuff the hat. Part 1 needs to be perfectly concave to sit on an Impkin's head.

Fasten off with yarn tail long enough to weave in.

Assembly

Pin in place on the head of the Impkin, sew to attach using the same color yarn as either the Impkin Body or Part 1 of the hat, and weave in the ends.

SHOULD YOUR IMPKIN SEEM QUIET OR NONCOMMUNICATIVE, CONSIDER—IMPKINS, LIKE ALL PEOPLE, COMMUNICATE IN COUNTLESS WAYS. PERHAPS YOUR IMPKIN COMMUNICATES WITH SOULFUL LOOKS OR BY FINDING AND BRINGING YOU GIFTS. SOME EVEN COMMUNICATE BY TRYING TO ENLIVEN YOUR DAY WITH GAMES—MOSTLY BY HIDING YOUR THINGS SO YOU CAN ENJOY SEEKING THEM OUT. DO YOUR BEST TO PLAY ALONG.

– Notes from the field, L. Mossgrove

FEATHER TOPPER (MAKE AS MANY AS YOU WANT)

Feather Ornament Color Yarn: Approximately 3 yd/2.75 m total

1. Starting with a long enough yarn tail to weave in later, Ch 6, starting in the second Ch from hook, HDC, DC, HDC, SC 2, Ch 1, Turn [5]
2. BLO [SC 3], Ch 6, Turn [3]
3. Starting in the second Ch from hook, HDC, DC 2, HDC 2, BLO [SC 3], Ch 1, Turn [8]
4. BLO [SC 3], Ch 3, Turn [3]

5. Starting in the second Ch from hook, HDC, DC, BLO [HDC, SC 2] [5]

Fasten off with 12 in/30.5 cm yarn tail.

Assembly

Pin in place on the head of the Impkin, sew to attach using the yarn tail, and weave in the ends.

SOME IMPKINS LIKE TO PRETEND THAT THEY ARE OTHER ANIMALS. IF YOU PROVIDE YOUR IMPKIN WITH FEATHERS, THEY MIGHT ACT LIKE A BIRD—I HAVE FOUND THEY QUITE ENJOY DOING A CHICKEN WALK. YOU NEED ONLY BECOME CONCERNED IF AND WHEN THEY TRY TO LAY EGGS.

HOWEVER, MANY A WINGED IMPKIN WILL AVOID FLYING IN FRONT OF THEIR PEOPLE. IT'S NOT THAT THEY AREN'T GRATEFUL FOR THEIR WINGS OR EXCITED TO SHOW THEM OFF; THEY'RE SIMPLY BEING POLITE TOWARD THE WINGLESS HUMANS IN THEIR LIVES.

– Notes from the field, L. Mossgrove

HORNS AND ANTLERS

Granting horns to Impkins provides an array of benefits, from helping them capture the resonance of music to giving them more ways to carry bags or wear jewelry. Many Impkins have expressed gratitude for the extra inch or two of height that horns provide. Just be aware you might sometimes have to shave them down a bit, should the horns grow unruly.

Impkins may have long or short, or wavy or pointy, horns and sometimes even antlers! A few rare Impkins have only one horn, and so some surmise they may be related to unicorns.

HORN AND ANTLER OPTIONS

Wide and Curled Horns

Short and Pointy Horns

Medium Wavy Horns

Large Antlers

Small Antlers

Unicorn Horn

WIDE AND CURLED HORNS (MAKE 1 OF EACH SIDE)

Any Color Yarn:
Approximately 18 yd/16.5 m total
(for 2)

First Side

1. SC 4 in Magic Circle, Sl St to beginning stitch, Ch 1 [4]

2. SC 4, Sl St to beginning stitch, Ch 1 [4]

3. Inc x 2, Dec, Sl St to beginning stitch, Ch 1 [5]

4. SC, Inc x 2, Dec, Sl St to beginning stitch, Ch 1 [6]

5. SC, Inc x 2, SC, Dec, Sl St to beginning stitch, Ch 1 [7]

6. SC 2, Inc x 2, SC, Dec, Sl St to beginning stitch, Ch 1 [8]

7. SC 2, Inc x 2, SC 2, Dec, Sl St to beginning stitch, Ch 1 [9]

8. SC 3, Inc x 2, SC 3, Skip 1 stitch, Sl St to beginning stitch, Ch 1 [10]

9. SC 3, Inc x 2, SC 3, Dec, Sl St to beginning stitch, Ch 1 [11]

10. SC 4, Inc x 2, SC 4, Skip 1 stitch, Sl St to beginning stitch, Ch 1 [12]

11. SC 4, Inc x 2, SC 4, Dec, Sl St to beginning stitch, Ch 1 [13]

12. SC 5, Inc x 2, SC 5, Skip 1 stitch, Sl St to beginning stitch, Ch 1 [14]

13. SC 5, Inc x 2, SC 5, Dec, Sl St to beginning stitch, Ch 1 [15]

14. SC 6, Inc x 2, SC 6, Skip 1 stitch, Sl St to beginning stitch, Ch 1 [16]

15. SC 6, Inc x 2, SC 6, Dec, Sl St to beginning stitch [17]

Fasten off with 12 in/30.5 cm yarn tail.

Second Side

1. SC 4 in Magic Circle, Sl St to beginning stitch, Ch 1 [4]

2. SC 4, Sl St to beginning stitch, Ch 1 [4]

3. 2 Dec in 3 SC, Triple SC Inc, Sl St to beginning stitch, Ch 1 [5]

4. Triple SC Dec, Inc, <Dec>, Inc, Sl St to beginning stitch, Ch 1 [6]

5. Dec, SC, Inc x 2, SC, Sl St to beginning stitch, Ch 1 [7]

6. Triple SC Dec, SC, Inc, <Dec>, Inc, SC, Sl St to beginning stitch, Ch 1 [8]

7. Dec, SC 2, Inc x 2, SC 2, Sl St to beginning stitch, Ch 1 [9]

8. Triple SC Dec, SC 2, Inc, <Dec>, Inc, SC 2, Sl St to beginning stitch, Ch 1 [10]

9. Dec, SC 3, Inc x 2, SC 3, Sl St to beginning stitch, Ch 1 [11]

10. Triple SC Dec, SC 3, Inc, <Dec>, Inc, SC 3, Sl St to beginning stitch, Ch 1 [12]

11. Dec, SC 4, Inc x 2, SC 4, Sl St to beginning stitch, Ch 1 [13]

12. Triple SC Dec, SC 4, Inc, <Dec>, Inc, SC 4, Sl St to beginning stitch, Ch 1 [14]

13. Dec, SC 5, Inc x 2, SC 5, Sl St to beginning stitch, Ch 1 [15]

14. Triple SC Dec, SC 5, Inc, <Dec>, Inc, SC 5, Sl St to beginning stitch, Ch 1 [16]

15. Dec, SC 6, Inc x 2, SC 6, Sl St to beginning stitch [17]

Fasten off with 12 in/30.5 cm yarn tail.

Assembly

Pin to attach to either side of the Impkin's head (it is optional to stuff the horns lightly with fiberfill—do not overstuff). Sew to attach using a yarn tail and weave in ends.

Standing Body
Style 1,
Arm Style 1,
Wide and Curled
Horns

SHORT AND POINTY HORNS (MAKE 2)

Any Color Yarn: Approximately 5 yd/4.5 m total (for 2)

1. SC 4 in Magic Circle, Sl St to beginning stitch, Ch 1 [4]
2. Inc, SC 3, Sl St to beginning stitch, Ch 1 [5]
3. SC 5, Sl St to beginning stitch, Ch 1 [5]
4. Inc, SC 4, Sl St to beginning stitch, Ch 1 [6]
5. Inc, SC 5, Sl St to beginning stitch, Ch 1 [7]
6. Inc, SC 6, Sl St to beginning stitch [8]

Fasten off with 12 in/30.5 cm yarn tail.

Assembly

Pin to attach to either side of the Impkin's head (it is optional to stuff the horns with fiberfill—if you do so, do it lightly). Sew to attach using a yarn tail and weave in ends.

MEDIUM WAVY HORNS (MAKE 2)

Any Color Yarn: Approximately 10 yd/9.25 m total (for 2)

1. Starting with a long enough yarn tail to weave in later, Ch 8, Sl St to the first Ch stitch, Ch 1 [8]

> When you work the SC stitches around the chain stitch spaces, you will not work into the individual chain stitches; instead, you will encase the chain stitches in the SC stitches you make.

2. SC 9 into the ring (working around the chain stitches and not into the individual chain stitches), Sl St to beginning stitch, Ch 1 [9]
3. SC 2, Inc, SC 3, Dec, SC, Sl St to beginning stitch, Ch 1 [9]
4. SC 6, Dec, SC, Sl St to beginning stitch, Ch 1 [8]
5. SC, Inc, SC 2, 2 Dec in 3 SC, SC, Sl St to beginning stitch, Ch 1 [8]
6. SC 5, 2 Dec in 3 SC, Sl St to beginning stitch, Ch 1 [7]
7. SC 2, Inc, SC 2, Dec, Sl St to beginning stitch, Ch 1 [7]
8. SC 6, Skip the last stitch, Sl St to beginning stitch, Ch 1 [6]
9. Dec, SC 2, <Dec>, SC 2, Sl St to beginning stitch, Ch 1 [6]
10. Dec, SC 4, Sl St to beginning stitch, Ch 1 [5]
11. Dec, SC, Inc, SC, Sl St to beginning stitch, Ch 1 [5]
12. Dec, SC 3, Sl St to beginning stitch [4]

Fasten off with 12 in/30.5 cm yarn tail, use the yarn tail to sew any remaining hole at the top of the Horn shut, thread the yarn tail down through the Horn, and use it to sew to attach to the head of the Impkin.

Assembly

Pin to attach to either side of the Impkin's head (it is optional to stuff the horns with fiberfill—if you do so, do it lightly). Sew to attach using a yarn tail and weave in ends.

LARGE ANTLERS (MAKE 2)

Any Color Yarn:
Approximately 33 yd/30.25 m
total (for 2)

Part 4: Make 1 Part 4 per antler, and set aside for reference once you reach Part 3

1. SC 5 in Magic Circle, Sl St to beginning stitch, Ch 1 [5]

2–4. (3 rows of) SC 5, Sl St to beginning stitch, Ch 1 [5]

5. SC 4, Inc, Sl St to beginning stitch, Ch 1 [6]

6. SC 6, Sl St to beginning stitch, Ch 1 [6]

7. SC 6, Sl St to beginning stitch [6]

Fasten off with short yarn tail.

Part 1

1. SC 5 in Magic Circle, Sl St to beginning stitch, Ch 1 [5]

2–4. (3 rows of) SC 5, Sl St to beginning stitch, Ch 1 [5]

5. SC 5, Sl St to beginning stitch [5]

Fasten off with short yarn tail.

Part 2

1. SC 5 in Magic Circle, Sl St to beginning stitch, Ch 1 [5]

2–3. (2 rows of) SC 5, Sl St to beginning stitch, Ch 1 [5]

4. SC, Dec, SC, Inc, Sl St to beginning stitch, Ch 1 [5]

5. SC 5, Sl St to beginning stitch, Ch 1 [5]

6. SC 3, start a Dec in the next stitch of Part 2 and complete it in the first stitch of the last row of Part 1, SC 3 in Part 1, start a Dec stitch in the last available stitch on Part 1 and complete it in the next available stitch on Part 2, Sl St to beginning stitch [8]

NOTE: Do not work into the "Sl St, Ch 1" join when attaching Part 1.

Fasten off with short yarn tail.

Part 3

1. SC 4 in Magic Circle, Sl St to beginning stitch, Ch 1 [4]

2–3. (2 rows of) SC 4, Sl St to beginning stitch, Ch 1 [5]

4. SC 3, Inc, Sl St to beginning stitch, Ch 1 [5]

5–6. (2 rows of) SC 5, Sl St to beginning stitch, Ch 1 [5]

7. SC 4, Inc, Sl St to beginning stitch, Ch 1 [6]

8–13. (6 rows of) SC 6, Sl St to beginning stitch, Ch 1 [6]

14. SC 2, start a Dec in the next available stitch on Part 3 and complete it in the second stitch on the final row of Part 2, working into the stitches of Part 2, Dec, SC 3, Dec, SC in the next available stitch on Part 3, Dec, Sl St to beginning stitch, Ch 1 [10]

NOTE: Do not work into the "Sl St, Ch 1" join when attaching Part 2.

15. SC 2, Dec, SC 3, Dec, SC, Sl St to beginning Stitch, Ch 1 [8]

16–18. (3 rows of) SC 8, Sl St to beginning stitch, Ch 1 [8]

19. SC 5, start a Dec stitch in the next available stitch and complete it into the fourth stitch on Part 4, SC 4 in Part 4, start a Dec in the last available stitch on Part 4 and finish in the next available stitch on current work, SC, Sl St to beginning stitch, Ch 1 [12]

NOTE: Do not work into the "Sl St, Ch 1" join when attaching Part 4.

20–23. (4 rows of) SC 12, Sl St to beginning stitch, Ch 1 [12]

24. (SC 2, Inc) x 4, Sl St to beginning stitch [16]

Fasten off with 12 in/30.5 cm yarn tail.

Assembly

You can lightly stuff the antlers. Alternatively, you can use a pipe cleaner inside the antlers to hold them up/shape them. These choices are both optional. Pin in place on the head of the Impkin, sew to attach using yarn tails, and weave in ends.

If you make more than one Impkin with large antlers, you may find that they engage in head-butting battles. Time-outs work well to discourage this behavior. Make sure to encourage them to really think about what they've done.

Standing Body Style 1, Arm Style 1, Large Antlers

SMALL ANTLERS (MAKE 2)

Any Color Yarn: Approximately 15 yd/13.75 m total (for 2)

Part 1: Make Part 1 first and set aside for reference once you reach Part 2

1. SC 4 in Magic Circle, Sl St to beginning stitch, Ch 1 [4]

2. SC 4, Sl St to beginning stitch, Ch 1 [4]

3. SC 3, Inc, Sl St to beginning stitch, Ch 1 [5]

4–5. (2 rows of) SC 5, Sl St to beginning stitch, Ch 1 [5]

Fasten off with short yarn tail.

Part 2

1. SC 4 in Magic Circle, Sl St to beginning stitch, Ch 1 [4]

2–3. (2 rows of) SC 4, Sl St to beginning stitch, Ch 1 [4]

4. SC 3, Inc, Sl St to beginning stitch, Ch 1 [5]

5–7. (3 rows of) SC 5, Sl St to beginning stitch, Ch 1 [5]

8. SC 3, Inc, SC, Sl St to beginning stitch, Ch 1 [6]

9–10. (2 rows of) SC 6, Sl St to beginning stitch, Ch 1 [6]

11. SC 2, start a Dec stitch in the next available stitch on Part 2 and complete the decrease in the fourth stitch on the final row of Part 1, SC 3 in Part 1, start a Dec stitch in the next available stitch on Part 1 and complete the decrease in the next available stitch on Part 2, SC 2, Sl St to beginning stitch, Ch 1 [9]

- -

NOTE: Do not work into the "Sl St, Ch 1" join when attaching Part 1.

- -

12. SC 3, Dec, SC 4, Sl St to beginning stitch, Ch 1 [8]

13. Inc, SC 2, Dec, SC 2, Inc, Sl St to beginning stitch, Ch 1 [9]

14. SC 9, Sl St to beginning stitch, Ch 1 [9]

15. SC 3, HDC 4, SC 2, Sl St to beginning stitch, Ch 1 [9]

Fasten off with 12 in/30.5 cm yarn tail.

Assembly

Pin in place on the head of the Impkin. Once you are satisfied with placement, sew to attach and weave in ends.

Standing Body
Style 1,
Arm Style 1,
Small Antlers

Standing Body
Style 1,
Arm Style 1,
Pony Ears,
Long, Curly Mane,
Unicorn Horn,
Pony Tail

AN IMPKIN UNICORN MAY SHOW SOME OF THE SAME BEHAVIORS AND DESIRES AS A REAL UNICORN. IT MIGHT FIND YOU WHEN YOU'RE SITTING DOWN AND PAW AT YOU UNTIL YOU START BRUSHING ITS MANE, OR IT MIGHT TRY TO STEAL ROSE PETALS FROM YOUR FLOWERS. IT MIGHT EVEN SNEAK THE OCCASIONAL CARROT! USUALLY, IT'S BETTER TO INDULGE THE IMPKINS IN THESE ODD LITTLE BEHAVIORS, LEST YOU ROB THEM OF THE ESSENCE OF UNICORN IN THEIR STUFFING. JUST BE CAREFUL IF YOU GIVE THEM ANY HOOVES!

– Notes from the field, L. Mossgrove

UNICORN HORN

Any Color Yarn:
Approximately 4 yd/3.75 m total

1. SC 5 in Magic Circle, continue in spiral [5]
2. BLO [SC 5] [5]
3. BLO [Inc, SC 4] [6]
4. BLO [SC 6] [6]
5. BLO [Inc, SC 5] [7]
6. BLO [SC 7] [7]
7. BLO [SC 7] [7]
8. BLO [Inc, SC 6] [8]
9. BLO [SC 8]

Fasten off with 12 in/30.5 cm yarn tail.

Assembly

You do not need to stuff the horn with fiberfill. Pin in place on the head of the Impkin. Once you are satisfied with placement, sew to attach and weave in ends.

SCALES

Some Impkins seem to be related to reptiles or the ancient dinosaurs (maybe dragons?), sporting scales down their back. If you choose to give your Impkin scales, keep watch for any reptilian tendencies. And if you give them wings, they will definitely start trying to breathe fire.

SCALE OPTIONS

Triangle Scales

Rounded Scales

TRIANGLE SCALES

Any Color Yarn:
Approximately 5 yd/4.5 m total

Starting with a long enough yarn tail to weave in later, (Ch 4, starting in the second Ch from hook, Sl St, SC, HDC); repeat as many times as you like to fit your Impkin [3]

> To reach from the center of the forehead to the tip of the Dinosaur/Dragon Tail, you can repeat the instructions 20 times.

Fasten off with 24 in/61 cm yarn tail.

Assembly

Pin in place. Once you are satisfied with placement, sew to attach using yarn tails and weave in ends.

ROUNDED SCALES

Any Color Yarn:
Approximately 5 yd/4.5 m total

Starting with a long enough yarn tail to weave in later, (Ch 5, starting in the fourth Ch from hook, DC, Half Trip); repeat as many times as you like to fit your Impkin [2]

> To reach from the center of the forehead to the tip of the Dinosaur/Dragon Tail, you can repeat the instructions 12 times.

Fasten off with 24 in/61 cm yarn tail.

Assembly

Pin in place. Once you are satisfied with placement, sew to attach using yarn tails and weave in ends.

TAILS

What sort of tail will your Impkin have, if any at all? Your Impkin will let you know which type they would prefer.

Tails can provide balance, an extra prehensile appendage, a way to signal an Impkin's delight, and a beautiful splash of color to chase them as they frolic. An Impkin will know just which kind of tail most matches their personality and their needs.

TAIL OPTIONS

Cat Tail

Dinosaur/Dragon Tail

Deer Tail

Pony Tail

Puppy Tail

Devil Tail

Stinger

Lion Tail

Bird Tail

CAT TAIL

Any Color Yarn:
Approximately 5 yd/4.5 m total

1. SC 6 in Magic Circle, Sl St to beginning stitch, Ch 1 [6]

2-4. (3 rows of) SC 6, Sl St to beginning stitch, Ch 1 [6]

5. SC, Inc, SC, 2 Dec in 3 SC, Sl St to beginning stitch, Ch 1 [6]

6. SC 2, <Dec>, SC 2, Dec, Sl St to beginning stitch, Ch 1 [6]

7-9. (3 rows of) SC 6, Sl St to beginning stitch, Ch 1 [6]

10. SC, 2 Dec in 3 SC, SC, Inc, Sl St to beginning stitch, Ch 1 [6]

11. SC, Dec, SC 2, <Dec>, SC, Sl St to beginning stitch, Ch 1 [6]

12-14. (3 rows of) SC 6, Sl St to beginning stitch, Ch 1 [6]

Fasten off with 12 in/30.5 cm yarn tail.

Assembly

Pin to attach to the back of the Impkin. Once you are satisfied with placement, sew to attach using the yarn tail and weave in ends.

DINOSAUR/DRAGON TAIL

Any Color Yarn:
Approximately 11 yd/10 m total

1. SC 6 in Magic Circle, Sl St to beginning stitch, Ch 1 [6]

2. SC 6, Sl St to beginning stitch, Ch 1 [6]

3. SC 5, Inc, Sl St to beginning stitch, Ch 1 [7]

4. SC 7, Sl St to beginning stitch, Ch 1 [7]

5. SC, HDC 4, SC 2, Sl St to beginning stitch, Ch 1 [7]

6. SC 6, <Dec>, SC, Sl St to beginning stitch, Ch 1 [8]

7. HDC 5, SC 3, Sl St to beginning stitch, Ch 1 [8]

8. SC 5, Inc, SC, Inc, Sl St to beginning stitch, Ch 1 [10]

9. SC, 2 Dec in 3 SC, SC 3, Inc, SC 2, Sl St to beginning stitch Ch 1 [10]

10. HDC 6, Inc, SC, Inc, HDC, Sl St to beginning stitch, Ch 1 [12]

11. SC 12, Sl St to beginning stitch, Ch 1 [12]

12. SC 7, Inc, SC, Inc, SC 2, Sl St to beginning stitch, Ch 1 [14]

13. HDC 8, Inc, SC, Inc, HDC 3, Sl St to beginning stitch, Ch 1 [16]

14. SC 2, Dec, SC 7, <Dec>, SC 5, Sl St to beginning stitch, Ch 1 [16]

15. SC 9, Inc, SC, Inc, SC 4, Sl St to beginning stitch, Ch 1 [18]

16. SC 18, Sl St to beginning stitch, Ch 1 [18]

17. HDC 10, Inc, SC, Inc, HDC 5, Sl St to beginning stitch, Ch 1 [20]

18. SC 11, Inc, SC, Inc, SC 6, Sl St to beginning stitch [22]

Fasten off with 18 in/45.75 cm yarn tail.

Assembly

1. Stuff medium-firm with fiberfill stuffing.

2. There are two options for attaching the tail: Pin to attach as is so that the tail sticks out straight from the body as shown.

Or fold the bottom of the tail into itself and pin to attach to the body so that the tail extends downward, as shown.

3. Sew to attach using yarn tail and weave in ends.

DEER TAIL

Any Color Yarn:
Approximately 7 yd/6.5 m total

1. SC 5 in Magic Circle, Sl St to beginning stitch, Ch 1 [5]

2. SC 2, Inc, SC 2, Sl St to beginning stitch, Ch 1 [6]

3. (SC, Inc) x 3, Sl St to beginning stitch, Ch 1 [9]

4. (SC 2, Inc) x 3, Sl St to beginning stitch, Ch 1 [12]

5. SC 12, Sl St to beginning stitch, Ch 1 [12]

6. SC 12, Sl St to beginning stitch, Ch 1 [12]

7. SC 12, Sl St to beginning stitch, Ch 1 [12]

8. (SC, Dec) x 4, Sl St to beginning stitch, Ch 1 [8]

9. Dec x 4, Sl St to beginning stitch [4]

Fasten off with 12 in/30.5 cm yarn tail. Lightly stuff or leave unstuffed, as desired.

Assembly

Pin in place on the tail area of the Impkin. Using yarn tails, sew to attach around the bottom edge and then, if desired, tack the top of the tail up to attach and weave in the ends.

PONY TAIL

Any Color Yarn:
Approximately 24 yd/22 m total

> For tight curls (as shown in photos), keep your chain stitches fairly tight.

1. Starting with a long enough yarn tail to weave in later, Ch 36, Turn, starting in the second Ch from hook, Inc x 34, SC, Ch 36, Turn [69]

2. Starting in the second Ch from hook, Inc x 35, SC in the first Ch from Row 1, Ch 36, Turn [71]

3. Starting in the second Ch from hook, Inc x 35, SC in the first Ch from Row 1, Ch 36, Turn [71]

4. Starting in the second Ch from hook, Inc x 35, SC in the first Ch from Row 1, Ch 36, Turn [71]

5. Starting in the second Ch from hook, Inc x 35, SC in the first Ch from Row 1, Ch 36, Turn [71]

6. Starting in the second Ch from hook, Inc x 35, SC in the first Ch from Row 1 [71]

Fasten off with 24 in/61 cm yarn tail.

Assembly

Pin in place on the tail area of the Impkin. Sew to attach using yarn tails and weave in the ends.

PUPPY TAIL

Any Color Yarn: Approximately 4 yd/3.75 m total

1. SC 6 in Magic Circle, Sl St to beginning stitch, Ch 1 [6]

2. SC 6, Sl St to beginning stitch, Ch 1 [6]

3. SC, Inc, SC, 2 Dec in 3 SC, Sl St to beginning stitch, Ch 1 [6]

4. SC 6, Sl St to beginning stitch, Ch 1 [6]

5. SC 6, Sl St to beginning stitch, Ch 1 [6]

6. SC, Inc, SC, 2 Dec in 3 SC, Sl St to beginning stitch, Ch 1 [6]

7. SC 6, Sl St to beginning stitch, Ch 1 [6]

8. SC 6, Sl St to beginning stitch, Ch 1 [6]

9. Dec, Inc, Inc, Dec, Sl St to beginning stitch [6]

Fasten off with 12 in/30.5 cm yarn tail.

Assembly

Pin in place on the tail area of the Impkin. Sew to attach using yarn tail and weave in the ends.

DEVIL TAIL

Any Color Yarn: Approximately 3 yd/2.75 m total

1. Starting with a long enough yarn tail to weave in later, Ch 22, Turn, starting in the third Ch from hook, HDC & DC & DC, Ch 2, Sl St in the second Ch from hook, working into the same stitch as the last DC, DC & DC & HDC, Ch 2, Sl St in the same stitch as the last HDC, Sl St 19 back along the OC [27]

Fasten off with 12 in/30.5 cm yarn tail.

Assembly

Pin in place on the tail area of the Impkin. Sew to attach using yarn tail and weave in the ends.

Standing Body
Style 1,
Arm Style 1,
Pony Ears,
Long, Curly Mane,
Unicorn Horn,
Pony Tail

STINGER

Any Color Yarn:
Approximately 3 yd/2.75 m total

1. SC 4 in Magic Circle, Sl St to beginning stitch, Ch 1 [4]

2. (SC, Inc) x 2, Sl St to beginning stitch, Ch 1 [6]

3. SC 6, Sl St to beginning stitch, Ch 1 [6]

4. (SC, Inc, SC) x 2, Sl St to beginning stitch, Ch 1 [8]

5. (SC 3, Inc) x 2, Sl St to beginning stitch [10]

Fasten off with 12 in/30.5 cm yarn tail.

Assembly

It is optional to stuff this piece with fiberfill. Pin to attach on the tail area of the Impkin. Sew to attach using the yarn tail and weave in the ends.

LION TAIL

Body Color Yarn:
Approximately 2 yd/1.75 m total

Accent Fur Color Yarn:
Approximately 1 yd/1 m total

Part 1: Body Color Yarn

Starting with a long enough yarn tail to weave in later, Ch 16, starting in the second Ch from hook, Sl St 15 [15]

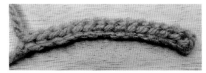

Fasten off with 12 in/30.5 cm yarn tail.

Part 2: Accent Fur Color Yarn

1. Cut 3 to 5 2-in/5-cm pieces of yarn.

2. Follow the instructions in the Short-Pieced Mane/Mohawk pattern on pages 90–91 for attaching the yarn to the end of the Part 1 tail.

3. Brush out the tiny tuft of yarn at the end of the tail.

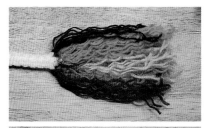

Assembly

Pin to attach the tail to the tail area of the Impkin. Sew to attach and weave in ends.

BIRD TAIL (MAKE 1 OR MORE)

Any Color Yarn:
Approximately 13 yd/12 m total

> In some of the following rows, you will not always use all of the available stitches/chains. These unworked stitches will be used in a later row.

1. Starting with a long enough yarn tail to weave in later, Ch 19, starting in the second Ch from hook, HDC, DC 2, HDC 3, SC 4, Ch 1, Turn [10]

> There will be 8 chain stitches left unworked after Row 1 is complete.

2. BLO [SC 8], Ch 6, Turn [8]
3. Starting in the second Ch from Hook, HDC, DC 2, HDC 2, BLO [HDC, SC 6, SC/HDC Dec & HDC], HDC, SC 2, Ch 1, Turn [17]

> There will be 4 chain stitches left unworked from Row 1 after Row 3 is complete.
>
> The SC/HDC Dec is worked down the "step" made by leaving stitches unworked in a previous row. Work into stitches as normal, not into the sides of stitches. The "&" symbol is defined in the Glossary.

4. BLO [SC 15], Ch 6, Turn [15]
5. Starting in the second Ch from hook, HDC, DC 2, HDC 2, BLO [HDC, SC 13, SC/HDC Dec & HDC], SC 3, Ch 1, Turn [24]

> Row 5 uses all remaining chain stitches from Row 1.

6. BLO [SC 22], Ch 6, Turn [22]
7. Starting in the second Ch from hook, HDC, DC 4, BLO [DC 4, HDC 6, SC 12], Ch 1, Turn [27]
8. BLO [SC 22], Ch 3, Turn [22]
9. Starting in the second Ch from hook, HDC, DC, BLO [DC, HDC 3, SC 13], Ch 1, Turn [19]

> There will be 5 stitches left unworked from Row 8 once Row 9 is complete.

10. BLO [SC 15], Ch 3, Turn [15]
11. Starting in the second Ch from hook, HDC, DC, BLO [DC, HDC 3, SC 6], Ch 1, Turn [12]

> There will be 5 stitches left unworked from Row 10 once Row 11 is complete.

12. BLO [SC 8], Ch 3, Turn [8]
13. Starting in the second Ch from hook, HDC, DC, BLO [DC, HDC 3, SC 3, SC/HDC Dec & HDC, SC 3, SC/HDC Dec & HDC, SC 4] [20]

> In Row 13, you will work into all remaining unworked stitches from previous rows.

Fasten off with 18 in/45.75 cm yarn tail.

Assembly

Pin to attach to the tail area of the Impkin. Sew to attach and weave in ends. You can make several pieces and attach to make a fuller, more peacock-like tail.

AN IMPKIN WITH PARTICULARLY VIBRANT AND EYE-CATCHING PLUMAGE WILL TEND TO SHOW IT OFF ALL THE TIME. THEY'LL FLASH IT IN FRONT OF YOU AND WAVE IT TO GET YOUR ATTENTION. BE SURE TO PERIODICALLY COMPLIMENT THEM, OR THEY'LL RESORT TO EVER MORE DRASTIC EFFORTS TO GAIN YOUR APPRECIATION.

– Notes from the field, L. Mossgrove

WINGS

If you happen to see your Impkin atop some bookshelf, clock, lamp, or chandelier, don't be alarmed! Impkins are fairly expert natural climbers, and they often enjoy getting a better vantage point on the world around them. You will discover their aptitudes at surprising times. Do take note, however: Even if they are given wings, they can have a hard time flying! Leave them to take to the air on their own time, if ever. If it is meant to be, they will find a way to soar!

WING OPTIONS

Fairy Wings

Feather Wings

Bat Wings

FAIRY WINGS

Any Color Yarn: Approximately 9 yd/8.25 m total

> This piece is worked in spiral, DO NOT "Sl St, Ch 1" at the end of Row 1.

1. Starting with a long enough yarn tail to weave in later, in Magic Circle: (SC 3, Ch 6) x 4 [12]

> The "Ch 2, Sl St in the second Ch from hook" instruction in Row 2's steps is used to create a picot or a little decorative point on each wing.

2A. Sl St 3, working into first Ch-6 space: SC, HDC, DC, Half Trip, Triple Crochet 4, Ch 2, Sl St in second Ch from hook, Triple Crochet 4, Half Trip, DC, HDC, SC [19 (20 with picot stitch included)]

> When you work the stitches around the chain stitch spaces, you will not work into the individual chain stitches; instead, you will encase the chain stitches in the stitches you make.

2B. Sl St 3, working into second Ch-6 space: SC, HDC 2, DC 4, Ch 2, Sl St in the second Ch from hook, DC 4, HDC 2, SC [17 (18 with picot stitch included)]

2C. Sl St 3, working into third Ch-6 space: SC, HDC 2, DC 4, Ch 2, Sl St in the second Ch from hook, DC 4, HDC 2, SC [17 (18 with picot stitch included)]

2D. Sl St 3, working into fourth Ch-6 space: SC, HDC, DC, Half Trip, Triple Crochet 4, Ch 2, Sl St in second Ch from hook, Triple Crochet 4, Half Trip, DC, HDC, SC, Sl St in the same stitch you first slip stitched into in 2A [19 (20 with picot stitch included)]

Fasten off with 18 in/45.75 cm yarn tail.

Assembly

Pin to attach. Using yarn tails, sew to attach and weave in ends.

Standing Body Style 1, Arm Style 1, Antennae Style 2, Stinger, Fairy Wings

FEATHER WINGS (MAKE 2)

Any Color Yarn:
Approximately 14 yd/12.75 m
total (for 2)

1. Starting with a long enough yarn tail to weave in later, Ch 4, Turn, starting in the second Ch from hook, HDC 3, Ch 1, Turn [3]

2. BLO [Inc, SC], Ch 3, Turn [3]

3. Starting in second Ch from hook, HDC 2, BLO [HDC, SC], Ch 1, Turn [4]

> There will be 1 stitch left unworked from the previous row.

4. BLO [SC 3], Ch 4, Turn [3]

5. Starting in the second Ch from hook, HDC 3, BLO [HDC, SC, SC/HDC Dec & HDC], Ch 1, Turn [7]

> The SC/HDC Dec is worked down the "step" made by leaving stitches unworked in a previous row.

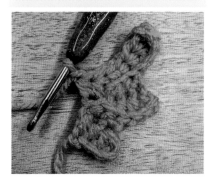

6. BLO [SC 6], Ch 4, Turn [6]

7. Starting in the second Ch from hook, HDC 3, BLO [HDC, SC 3], Ch 1, Turn [7]

> There will be 2 stitches left unworked from the previous row.

8. BLO [SC 6], Ch 4, Turn [6]

9. Starting in the second Ch from hook, HDC 3, BLO [HDC 3, SC 2, SC/HDC Dec & HDC, HDC], Ch 1, Turn [11]

10. BLO [SC 8], Ch 5, Turn [8]

Standing Body Style 2, Arm Style 2, Feather Wings

11. Starting in the second Ch from hook, HDC 4, BLO [HDC 2, SC 3], Ch 1, Turn [9]

> There will be 3 stitches left unworked from the previous row.

12. BLO [SC 6], Ch 3, Turn [6]

13. Starting in the second Ch from hook, HDC 2, BLO [HDC 4, SC, SC/HDC Dec & HDC, HDC, SC], Ch 1 [11]

14. Reorient work and starting by working into the same stitch you last single crocheted into in Row 13, SC along the unfinished wing edge back to the OC (approximately 10 SC) [~10]

Fasten off with 24 in/61 cm yarn tail.

Assembly

Pin to attach to the back of the Impkin. Use yarn tails to sew to attach and weave in ends.

BAT WINGS (MAKE 1 LEFT WING AND 1 RIGHT WING)

Accent Color Yarn: Approximately 14 yd/12.75 m total (for 2)

Main Body Color Yarn: Approximately 6 yd/5.5 m total (for 2)

Part 1: Accent Color Yarn

1. Starting with a long enough yarn tail to weave in later, Ch 7, Turn, starting in the second Ch from hook, SC 4, Dec, Ch 1, Turn [5]

2. Dec, SC 3, Ch 4, Turn [4]

3. Starting in the second Ch from hook and working back along the chain stitches and then the other stitches from Row 2, SC 7, Ch 1, Turn [7]

4. SC 4, Ch 1, Turn [4]

> In this and following rows, you will not always use all available stitches/chains. These unworked stitches will be used in a later row. There will be 3 stitches left unworked from the previous row.

5. SC 3, Inc, Ch 1, Turn [5]

6. SC 2, Ch 1, Turn [2]

> There will be 3 stitches left unworked from the previous row.

7. SC, Inc, Ch 1, Turn [3]

8. SC 2, SC/HDC Dec & HDC, SC, SC/HDC Dec & HDC, SC, Sl St, Ch 1, Turn [9]

> The SC/HDC Dec is worked down the "step" made by leaving stitches unworked in a previous row. Work into stitches as normal, not into the sides of stitches.

9. Skip the Sl St, BLO [SC 6, Dec], Ch 1, Turn [7]

> All indicated stitches should be worked as BLO for the Right Wing and FLO for the Left Wing.

10. SC 4, Ch 1, Turn [4]

> There will be 3 stitches left unworked from the previous row.

11. SC 3, Inc, Ch 1, Turn [5]

12. SC 2, Ch 1, Turn [2]

> There will be 3 stitches left unworked from the previous row.

13. SC, Inc, Ch 1, Turn [3]

14. SC 2, SC/HDC Dec & HDC, SC, SC/HDC Dec & HDC, SC, Sl St in the same spot you slip stitched into at the end of Row 8, Ch 1, Turn [9]

15. Skip the Sl St, BLO [SC 6, Dec], Ch 1, Turn [7]

All indicated stitches should be worked as BLO for the Right Wing and FLO for the Left Wing.

16. SC 4, Ch 1, Turn [4]

There will be 3 stitches left unworked from the previous row.

17. SC 3, Inc, Ch 1, Turn [5]

18. SC 2, Ch 1, Turn [2]

There will be 3 stitches left unworked from the previous row.

19. SC, Inc, Ch 1, Turn [3]

20. SC 2, SC/HDC Dec & HDC, SC, SC/HDC Dec & HDC, SC, Sl St in the same spot you slip stitched into at the end of Row 14 [9]

Fasten off with 12 in/30.5 cm yarn tail.

Part 2: Body Color Yarn

The stiffer the yarn you use for Part 2, the better. The wings will hold themselves up. You do not need to use the Body Color Yarn if you would prefer to use a stiffer/bulkier yarn. You can also size down your hook to make your stitches a little bit tighter to increase the stiffness of this piece. These techniques will all help the wings stand up on their own. If you would like to, you CAN use wire in this row to give the wings pose-ability and strength. If this is an item intended as a toy, do not use wire. If you use wire, use a light, 18-gauge, cloth-wrapped wire, hold it along the edge of the wing, and crochet all stitches around the wire as you work along the edge.

1. Starting with a long enough yarn tail to weave in later, attach the yarn to the side of the first SC from Row 1 of Part 1. Working along the edge of the wing toward where you fastened off Part 1, SC along the edge till you reach the point (this point is the elbow of the wing), work an Inc in the point, SC to the end of the wing edge, Ch 1, Turn

2. Sl St back along the stitches from Row 1 until you slip stitch into the first available SC in the Inc you made in Row 1 into the elbow point, then SC along the first available ridge of BLO or FLO stitches to the end, and then Ch 1, Turn

3. Sl St back along the SC stitches from Row 2, Sl St again in the same first SC of the Inc in the elbow point of the wing, Sl St in the second SC in the Inc in the elbow point of the wing, then SC along the next available BLO or FLO ridge of stitches to the end, and then Ch 1, Turn

4. Sl St back along the SC stitches from Row 3, Sl St again in the same second SC in the Inc in the elbow point of the wing, and then Sl St back along the edge of the wing to where you started Part 2

Fasten off with 18 in/45.75 cm yarn tail.

Assembly

Pin to attach to the back of the Impkin. Sew to attach using yarn tails and weave in ends.

CLOTHING

A little vest or a tutu can make an Impkin very happy! For a reclusive type, try making them a shell, and they will love you forever.

Also, providing an Impkin with their own garb makes it far less likely to go rooting through your own drawers and closets to find accessories. Many an Impkin's person has found their Impkin wearing a sock as a hat and lamented their failure to provide adequate clothing.

CLOTHING OPTIONS

Short Vest

Tutu

Turtle Shell

SHORT VEST

Any Color Yarn:
Approximately 7 yd/6.5 m total

1. Starting with a long enough yarn tail to weave in later, Ch 16, Turn, starting in the second Ch from hook, SC 15, Ch 1, Turn [15]

2. HDC 15, Ch 1, Turn [15]

3. HDC 15, Ch 2, Turn [15]

> The Ch 2 here is just a turning chain. Do not crochet into it in the following row.

4. DC 2, Ch 3, skip 3 stitches, DC 5, Ch 3, skip 3 stitches, DC 2, Ch 1, Turn [9]

5. Dec, SC 3 around the chain stitches, SC 5, SC 3 around the chain stitches, Dec [13]

> When you work the stitches around the chain stitch spaces, you will not work into the individual chain stitches; instead, you will encase the chain stitches in the stitches you make.

6. Continue crocheting in the same direction down the unfinished side of the vest toward the OC, starting in the same stitch your last Dec ended in, SC about 7 to the corner, Inc in the corner, SC 13 along the bottom edge of the vest, Inc in the corner, SC about 7 back up to the first Dec worked in Row 5, Sl St [~31]

Fasten off with 12 in/30.5 cm yarn tail.

Assembly

Weave in the ends. And, if they consent, dress your Impkin in their new vest.

TUTU

Any Color Yarn:
Approximately 21 yd/19.25 m total

1. Starting with a long enough yarn tail to weave in later, Ch 29, starting in the second Ch from hook, (SC, Inc) x 14, Ch 1, Turn [42]

2. (SC, Inc) x 21, Ch 1, Turn [63]

3. (SC, Inc) x 31, SC, Ch 1, Turn [94]

4. (SC, Inc) x 47 [141]

Fasten off with 12 in/30.5 cm yarn tail.

Assembly

Wrap the chain side of this piece around the waist of the Impkin. Pin in place. Once you are satisfied with placement, sew to attach, sew the ends of the skirt together, and weave in ends.

TURTLE SHELL

Any Color Yarn:
Approximately 13 yd/12 m total

1. SC 8 in Magic Circle, Sl St to beginning stitch, Ch 1 [8]

2. Inc x 8, Sl St to beginning stitch, Ch 1 [16]

3. HDC, HDC Inc, (SC, Inc) x 2, (HDC, HDC Inc) x 2, (SC, Inc) x 2, HDC, HDC Inc, Sl St to beginning stitch, Ch 1 [24]

4. HDC, HDC Inc, HDC, (SC, Inc, SC) x 2, (HDC, HDC Inc, HDC) x 2, (SC, Inc, SC) x 2, HDC, HDC Inc, HDC, Sl St to beginning stitch, Ch 1 [32]

5. HDC 3, HDC Inc, (SC 3, Inc) x 2, (HDC 3, HDC Inc) x 2, (SC 3, Inc) x 2, HDC 3, HDC Inc, Sl St to beginning stitch, Ch 1 [40]

6. FLO [Sl St 40], Sl St to beginning stitch, Ch 1 [40]

7. Working into the leftover BLO stitches from Row 5, BLO [SC 40], Sl St to beginning stitch [40]

Fasten off with 24 in/61 cm yarn tail.

Assembly

Pin to attach the Shell to the back of the Impkin. Position it carefully; once you are satisfied with placement, sew to attach and weave in the ends.

NECK ORNAMENTATION

Impkins can get cold out in the wild,
so make yours a scarf for protection
from the wind. They also like to feel
dapper with a necktie or bow tie.

NECK ORNAMENTATION OPTIONS

Scarf

Bow Tie

Necktie

SCARF

Any Color Yarn:
Approximately 14 yd/12.75 m total

1. Starting with a long enough yarn tail to weave in later, Ch 5, Turn, starting in the second Ch from hook, SC 4, Ch 1, Turn [4]

2-50. (49 rows of) SC 4, Ch 1, Turn [4]

Fasten off with 12 in/30.5 cm yarn tail. You can sew to attach to the neck of the Impkin, but you can also designate this piece as a removable accessory.

Cut 12 pieces of the same yarn in 3 in/7.5 cm lengths. Use slipknots to attach to the stitches/chains of the first and last rows of the scarf. Pull apart the twist of the yarn to make it look like fringe. Trim to desired length.

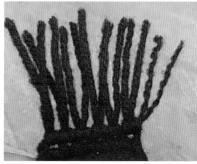

Sitting Body Style 2, Arm Style 2, Scarf

Sitting Body
Style 1,
Arm Style 2,
Top Hat, Bow Tie

BOW TIE

Any Color Yarn:
Approximately 2 yd/1.75 m

1. Starting with a long enough yarn tail to weave in later, Ch 6, starting in the second Ch from hook, HDC 2, Ch 1, Skip 1 Ch stitch, HDC 2, Ch 1, Turn [4]

2. HDC 2, SC around the Ch 1 and the Skipped Ch stitch, HDC 2 [5]

Fasten off with 12 in/30.5 cm yarn tail.

Assembly

Pin in place on the neck of the Impkin. Sew to attach using yarn tails and weave in the ends.

**Standing Body
Style 1,
Arm Style 1,
Necktie**

NECKTIE

Any Color Yarn:
Approximately 3 yd/2.75 m

1. Starting with a long enough yarn tail to weave in later, Ch 11, starting in the second Ch from hook, Sl St, HDC, DC 2, HDC 2, SC 3, Special Bobble Stitch, Ch 12 [9]

Work the Special Bobble Stitch as follows: YO, insert your hook in the next available stitch, YO, pull up, YO, insert your hook in the same stitch, YO, pull up, YO, insert your hook in the same stitch, YO, pull up, YO, pull through all remaining loops.

Fasten off with 18 in/45.75 cm yarn tail.

Assembly

Pin in place on the neck of the Impkin. The first part of Row 1 is the front of the Necktie; the final chain of Row 1 should wrap around the neck of the Impkin. Sew to attach using the yarn tail and weave in the ends.

AT SOME POINT, YOUR IMPKIN MIGHT START COPYING YOU IN YOUR PROFESSIONAL ENDEAVORS. IF YOU GO INTO AN OFFICE, THEY WILL ASK TO COME AS WELL. IF YOU TYPE AT A KEYBOARD, THEY MIGHT TRY TO MAKE THEIR OWN OUT OF CARDBOARD AND TAP AWAY. IT'S BEST FOR THEM IF YOU HELP AND ENCOURAGE THEM TO PURSUE THEIR PROFESSIONAL TASTES AS MUCH AS YOU CAN; YOU WOULDN'T WANT TO DISCOURAGE THEM!

– Notes from the field, L. Mossgrove

ACCESSORIES

*Impkins often have special treasures
to hide. You may wish to make a bag
for them to hide their trinkets.*

ACCESSORY OPTIONS

Backpack

Messenger Bag

BACKPACK

Any Color Yarn:
Approximately 12 yd/11 m total

1. Starting with a long enough yarn tail to weave in later, SC 6 in Magic Circle, Sl St to beginning stitch, Ch 1 [6]

2. Inc x 6, Sl St to beginning stitch, Ch 1 [12]

3. (SC, Inc) x 6, Sl St to beginning stitch, Ch 1 [18]

4–8. (5 rows of) SC 18, Sl St to beginning stitch, Ch 1 [18]

9. (HDC, Ch 1, skip 1 stitch) x 9, Sl St to beginning stitch [18]

> The chain stitches are counted in the stitch count for Row 9 only in this section.

10. (Ch 12, Sl St in the first stitch on Row 9) x 2, Ch 1, starting in the first stitch on Row 9, (HDC, HDC 2 around the Ch 1 stitch space) x 9, Sl St to beginning HDC stitch [27]

Fasten off with 12 in/30.5 cm yarn tail.

Assembly

1. Weave in the end.

2. Cut a piece of yarn that is 12 in/30.5 cm long. Weave this piece of yarn through the openings in the skipped stitches from Row 9 on the Backpack. Pull this yarn tight to close the backpack and tie in a bow to close.

3. Put the Impkin's Arms through the loops on the Backpack created in Row 10 so that the Impkin can wear the Backpack.

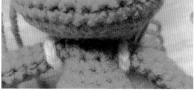

Periodically check their backpack to be sure they're not making off with anything small and shiny without you knowing about it.

MESSENGER BAG

Any Color Yarn:
Approximately 7 yd/6.5 m total

1. Starting with 18 in/30.5 cm yarn tail, Ch 9, starting in the second Ch from hook, SC 7, Inc, continue to crochet around to the other side of the starting chain, SC 6, SC in the same chain stitch as your first SC in this row, Sl St to beginning stitch, Ch 1 [16]

2. BLO [SC 16], Sl St to beginning stitch, Ch 1 [16]

3–5. (3 rows of) SC 16, Sl St to beginning stitch, Ch 1 [16]

Sitting Body
Style 2,
Arm Style 2,
Small Antlers, Scarf,
Messenger Bag

6. SC 8, Ch 28, Sl St in the first SC you worked in this row, Ch 1 [8]

> The Ch 28 in Row 6 creates the Messenger Bag strap. You can adjust the number of chains to be longer or shorter as needed.

7. Working into the 8 SC from Row 6 (if necessary, turn to work along these stitches), BLO [SC 8], Ch 1, Turn [8]

8. FLO [SC 8], Ch 1, Turn [8]

9. SC 8, Ch 1, Turn [8]

10. SC 8, Ch 1, Turn [8]

11. SC 8 [8]

Fasten off with 12 in/30.5 cm yarn tail.

Assembly

1. If you want to tie the Messenger Bag closed, you can weave the ending yarn tail through the edge of the last row to the center of the last row, and you can weave the starting yarn tail through the inside of the Messenger Bag to the center/bottom of the Messenger Bag. Then you can use the 2 yarn tails to tie a small bow, which will keep the bag closed.

2. If you do not want to tie the Messenger Bag closed, you can weave in the ends.

3. Sling the bag over the Impkin's shoulder; it is easiest to do this by inserting the feet-end of the Impkin through the Messenger Bag strap.

ACKNOWLEDGMENTS

Special thanks to my husband and best friend, Greg, without whom I could not have accomplished all that I have. Thank you for learning to crochet. Thank you for encouraging me. I love you.

To my children, Riley and Harper, my little nut and my golubushka. I love you.

Special thanks to my brother, Brendan Conway, who supported me through the process of creating this book, and to my wonderful sister-in-law, Grace Jacobson. Brendan is also the writer behind filling out the details and world of the Impkins. Thank you, Brendan, for giving us a deeper glimpse into the lives of these little creatures.

Thank you to my parents, Velma Conway and Richard Conway, and to my in-laws, Joy Lapp and Jim Lapp, for all your love and support.

Special thanks to Jen Starbird and Sarah Constein for being friends, moderating my FB group, testing patterns, and helping to make this book the best it can be.

Additional special thanks to Tammy Simmons and Amie Fournier-Flather for jumping in wholeheartedly to help with editing in addition to moderating on Facebook and being wonderful, supportive human beings.

Some Impkins were made and photographed by Lauren Lewis, including the cover image. She also did a beautiful job crocheting, taming, and photographing the monster on the following preview page to debut the next book! Special thanks to her for doing a fantastic job and always using her personal brand of magic to bring my creations to life in a very special way.

For more information, you can go here: https://www.facebook.com/handmadebylaurenlewis
Or here: https://www.instagram.com/handmadebylaurenlewis
Or here: https://www.ravelry.com/people/MadeByLaurenLewis

Special thanks to my FB group moderators and friends:

Morgan Carpuski	Laci Lynn Hall	Jade Asli Muyan
Sarah Constein	Dayna Lynn Inouye	Laura Owens
Shawna Dresslar	Kate Jacques	Tammy Simmons
Heather Flint	Daniel Jagoda	Jen Starbird
Amie Fournier-Flather	Elizabeth Keane	Jennifer Steyn
Alix Frere	Lauren Lewis	Jasmine Winston
Jeremy Leon Guerrero	Laura Marshall	

Special thanks to my agent a.k.a. Book Doula, Christi Cardenas.

COMING IN 2024:
CROCHET MONSTERS!